DATE DUE

Demco, Inc. 38-293

DEC 1 1 200

THE NBC ADVISORY COUNCIL AND RADIO PROGRAMMING, 1926–1945

NBC Advisory Council and Radio Programming, 1926–1945

Louise M. Benjamin

Southern Illinois University Press
Carbondale

Printed in the United States of America

12   11   10   09   4   3   2   1

Library of Congress Cataloging-in-Publication Data
Benjamin, Louise Margaret.
The NBC Advisory Council and radio program-
ming, 1926–1945 / Louise M. Benjamin.
  p. cm.
Includes bibliographical references and index.
ISBN-13: 978-0-8093-2919-9 (cloth : alk. paper)
ISBN-10: 0-8093-2919-0 (cloth : alk. paper)
1. NBC Advisory Council. 2. Radio broadcasting
policy—United States—History—20th century.
3. Radio broadcasting—Social aspects—United
States. I. Title.
PN1991.3.U6B46 2009
384.540973—dc22   2008051363

Printed on recycled paper. ♻
The paper used in this publication meets the minimum requirements of American National Standard
for Information Sciences—Permanence of Paper for
Printed Library Materials, ANSI Z39.48-1992. ∞

I dedicate this book to
all my teachers at Whiting Community School,
especially Mary Baker, Genevieve Baker,
and Dorothy Bridgford.

Contents

Preface

THIS BOOK'S BEGINNINGS CAN BE TRACED TO THE MID-1980s, when I had the pleasure of interviewing Everett Needham Case and Josephine Young Case. Then in his eighties, Case had been secretary to Owen Young, CEO of General Electric and the Radio Corporation of America. He also served as the recording secretary for NBC's Advisory Council and had married Young's daughter, Josephine. I was talking with both of them about Young's contributions to radio in the 1920s, especially regulatory policies.

In the course of our conversation, I mentioned NBC's Advisory Council and the observation of other historians that the council's mission was largely ceremonial. Mr. Case smiled and said that perception was inaccurate. He said he remembered discussions revolving around broadcast of a variety of contentious issues led by Charles Evans Hughes and Elihu Root—"Why, he was as old then as I am now," he said as he smiled, then added, "and what an intellect he had." As we continued chatting about Owen Young, early radio, and these long-ago controversial issues, I realized far more existed to the story of early radio and the influence of NBC's Advisory Council than previous historians had noted. Thus the seeds for this book were planted and now have come to fruition.

As I visited archives over the next decade, I located numerous materials regarding the council and its activities. Since publication of my first book on early radio, *Freedom of the Air and the Public Interest: First Amendment Rights in Broadcasting to 1935*, in 2001, I began working in earnest to compile the documentation for this manuscript. Archivists too numerous to mention helped me locate resources used here. I especially thank the gracious individuals who work at the AT&T Archives in Warren, New Jersey; the Herbert Hoover Presidential Library in West Branch, Iowa; Kansas State Libraries in Manhattan, Kansas; the Seely Mudd Library at Princeton University in Princeton, New Jersey; the St. Lawrence University Libraries in Canton, New York; the Wisconsin State Historical Society in Madison; the University of Maryland Libraries in College Park; and the National Archives and the Library of Congress in Washington, D.C., for their generous assistance.

Thanks also go to the University of Georgia's Jane and Harry Willson Center for Humanities and Arts and its director, Betty Jean Craige, for financial and moral support. Over the years my colleagues at Kansas State University, the University of Georgia, and Indiana University also offered encouragement and advice during the sometimes frustrating "archival digging" and "laborious writing" stages of this project. I thank them for their insight and assistance. My editors at Southern Illinois University Press, especially Wayne Larsen, offered excellent suggestions as this manuscript proceeded through the publication process. I am grateful to them for their efforts in improving my prose.

Last, but not least, I thank all my teachers from kindergarten through graduate school. Each of you has helped cultivate the intellectual curiosity that has led to my academic career. I especially recognize my early teachers at Whiting Community School, especially Mary Baker, Genevieve Baker, and Dorothy Bridgford. "Miss Baker" taught me basic reading and writing in kindergarten. My fascination with words and the meanings they convey began there. In addition to being my wonderful sixth grade teacher, "Mrs. Baker" tutored me during my fifth- and sixth-grade years when I was recovering from back surgery. In junior high and high school "Mrs. Bridgford" nurtured in me a great respect for the power of the English language. Any mangling of the written word in this book, however, is completely my own doing. To these wise teachers, as well as the others at Whiting Community School who taught me, I dedicate this book.

THE NBC ADVISORY COUNCIL AND RADIO PROGRAMMING, 1926–1945

An Overview: The Evolution of RCA and Radio Programming

TODAY, BROADCAST AND ELECTRONIC MEDIA content is affected by a number of factors: program costs, technological improvements, development of new formats, the cloning of successful shows, overall competition for audience attention and leisure time, and changes in audience tastes and preferences, to name a few. But, in the early 1920s, radio programming was rudimentary, improvised, and crude, voraciously devouring talent and their routines at an unprecedented rate. In these early years, radio often caught whatever events and speakers it could.[1] In 1921 radio station KDKA's first regular announcer, Harold W. Arlin, relied "heavily on playing borrowed phonograph records, reading news headlines and community service bulletins, and giving extended explanations of the Arlington time signals" carried by the Navy's radio station in Virginia.[2]

In his biography, WJZ announcer Norman Brokenshire noted that in radio's first few years, the station had a program if performers dropped by the studio. While fixed scheduling of speakers and programs was standard by the mid-1920s for stations in large markets, if acts failed to materialize, an announcer was stuck with filling airtime. One day, three back-to-back acts did not show up for Brokenshire's shift. After filling with a lot of improvised material, Brokenshire finally announced to his audience, "Now, here are the sounds of the city" and hung a microphone out the window.[3]

During the early 1920s, religious programs, musical concerts, stage productions, and sporting events found their way onto the air and presaged later radio program developments. For instance, the 1921 heavyweight boxing championship between Jack Dempsey and Georges Carpentier and the World Series between the New York Giants and the New York Yankees drew large audiences, foretelling future development of the profitable sports programming genre. Opera and orchestras provided live entertainment, and recordings often filled much of a station's airtime.[4]

Before 1923, no formal programs existed. Show openings and closings had yet to be devised, and exact or even approximate program timing was absent. Talent was not paid, and no regular, week-after-week or daily programs were scheduled. Programs were often "one-timers," because the concepts of regularly scheduled programs and repeated episodes were yet to come. Studios broadcast talks and light music. Vocals were solos or small groups. During 1922 and 1923, larger stations in metropolitan areas began using the latest technological developments for remote pickup of orchestras from hotels and other venues. Plays and opera were carried from the stage, and sporting events were occasionally aired as stunts to attract attention to stations. While some facilities broadcast weather forecasts and informational bulletins, regular newscasts were nonexistent. Few stations were on the air more than three or four hours per day, and many were on the air five hours or fewer *per week*. In general, few broadcasters went on the air at the same time each day.[5]

By 1925 the novelty of the medium had worn off, and radio was fast becoming a household necessity. Receiver technology had improved, and listeners demanded increasing sophistication and diversity in programs and formats. By the time the National Broadcasting Company (NBC) went on the air in November 1926 as the first permanent national network, program formats recognizable today had begun to evolve in large metropolitan areas. Many shows now had an open and a close and ran on regular schedules, with quarter-hour, half-hour, or hour-length programs common. Stations also made extensive use of announcer-narrators and began to build programs around ideas and themes.[6]

As shows evolved to the delight of listeners, behind-the-scenes actions influenced what they heard. Economic interests, regulatory issues, business competition, and technological advances shaped programming, and affecting these concerns was a very real apprehension of corporate dominance over the medium, including programming. These fears led companies and the government to adopt various measures to diffuse anxiety and combat potential monopolistic tendencies. One measure General Electric (GE) and the Radio Corporation of America (RCA) adopted when developing NBC was the incorporation of a board of independent advisers to assist in program development and to review complaints of program censorship and control.

This book is the story of that group—the NBC Advisory Council—and its influence over radio program evolution from the council's much publicized inception in 1926 until it quietly disbanded in 1945. To appreciate the council's importance to both NBC and the public, a general understanding of RCA's development and a grasp of overall radio programming during this time period are essential. The balance of this chapter details both.

Formation of RCA and NBC

The story of the birth and growth of RCA has been told often,[7] but a brief overview is necessary to understand the rationale and need for the NBC Advisory Council. In April 1919, when federal legislation that would have granted the Navy control over all radio in the post–World War I years failed, Navy officers in charge of radio, W. H. G. Bullard and S. C. Hooper, met with General Electric managers to ask GE to refrain from selling or granting any of its patent rights to the Marconi Company, based in Great Britain. At the time, GE was engaged in discussions with Marconi over rights that the Navy feared would give Marconi a virtual monopoly over worldwide wired and wireless communication, to the detriment of American national defense and commercial interests.[8]

In addition, the Navy wanted GE to develop an American communication company strong enough to establish and maintain a dominant position for the United States in radio communications. At the Navy's insistence, Owen Young, then one of GE's attorneys, suspended negotiations with Marconi and began investigating the patent situation to see whether American firms could be brought together to form an American-based company without violating the antimonopoly clauses of the Sherman and Clayton Antitrust Acts. Young also knew that to achieve the goals outlined by the Navy, American Marconi would have to be persuaded to turn over its assets to any newly formed corporation. GE, under Young's direction, began negotiations with British Marconi in the summer of 1919 for purchase of its American subsidiary, a move that greatly pleased government agencies, especially the Navy.[9]

During negotiations, Young warned Marconi's corporate officers that the U.S. Congress might nationalize radio because of the government's fears of foreign control over American communication. Neither GE nor British Marconi wanted that possibility to materialize, so over the summer they hammered out an agreement in which GE acquired American Marconi's assets and agreed to put $4 million into the new company in exchange for preferred stock at par value. GE also agreed to turn over all its existing radio patents and those it developed during the next twenty-five years to the new radio corporation. Overall, these negotiations gave GE 59 percent of the common stock in the new company, the Radio Corporation of America.[10]

By late fall 1919, Owen Young was assuring Congress that the purpose of this new, thoroughly American company was to develop radio communication, not only in the United States but wherever American business was large enough to demand it, especially South America. In a letter, he guaranteed Senator Miles Poindexter, chairman of the Senate Committee on Naval Affairs, that the new company was not seeking a monopoly in the field of radio communication. To placate Secretary of the Navy Josephus Daniels, Young also wrote Poindexter that RCA had a favorable attitude toward government regulatory control over radio. In reality, however, Young knew the likelihood of naval control over radio was remote, as the postwar Congress was one that did not favor such regulation.[11]

During the late teens and early twenties, AT&T, RCA, GE, Westinghouse, and United Fruit Company signed agreements allowing all signatories to exchange patents and scientific developments regarding radio. Known as "patent pooling," these agreements were made largely at the Navy's insistence so that the military could benefit from the most advanced radio equipment available. The companies themselves realized an exchange of patents would allow them to shape an expanding radio business, but they worried that with these contractual agreements would come charges of monopolistic, anticompetitive actions.

Trying to discern future government reactions, RCA and GE officials met with Attorney General Mitchell Palmer during the waning days of the Woodrow Wilson administration. Later, after Warren Harding's election, they met with Palmer's successor, Harry Daugherty. During both meetings, RCA-GE representatives stressed the need for the military to have the latest equipment for defense. Both attorneys general stated that it was the longstanding policy of the attorney general's office not to express opinions on the legality of proposed arrangements. But both men tacitly gave their approval to RCA's patent pool. In the 1920 meeting, Palmer was quick to give his unspoken approval to the arrangement through indicating to the companies that the "agreement looked like an excellent business arrangement." In 1921 Daugherty stated no hasty charges of monopoly would ever be taken during his watch.[12]

In spite of these assurances, investigations came. In 1923 Congress asked the Federal Trade Commission (FTC) to investigate the radio industry for monopolistic practices, and the subsequent investigation led to a formal complaint against the signatory companies to the 1920 patent pooling agreement. FTC hearings and scrutiny of the industry lasted until 1928, when the FTC dropped the complaint. In the meantime, the patent pooling agreements collapsed into a vicious, mammoth intercompany struggle over broadcasting. Because the 1920 contract did not specify who could broadcast and under what conditions, the companies began intense, ultrasecret discussions in 1924 to clarify their rights. In the background, hovering over their urgent, clandestine talks was the FTC investigation.[13]

The companies were determined to resolve their internecine war without government knowledge or oversight and had aligned themselves into two camps—the Radio Group (GE, RCA, Westinghouse) and the Telephone Group (AT&T and its subsidiary, Western Electric). Each group thought it had the sole right to develop the lucrative broadcast business. Because they had reached an impasse in their own negotiations, the companies finally agreed to binding arbitration and looked to one referee, Roland W. Boyden, a noted jurist, to decide their epic clash. Boyden heard arguments for each side and mulled over testimony and documents for months. In November 1924 he sent a draft of his opinion to each party to give the disputants the opportunity to object. The Radio Group was elated, as on point after point, Boyden upheld its position. Both factions filed comments with Boyden, but neither changed the substance of the draft, and in March 1925, Boyden issued his final, binding ruling.[14]

At this point, the Telephone Group played its trump card. John W. Davis, a recent candidate for the U.S. presidency and one of the authors of the Clayton Antitrust Act (and later member of the Advisory Council), wrote a consultative memorandum to the Radio Group from the Telephone Group. It stated that if the patent pooling agreements meant what Boyden said they meant, then much of the pact was, and had always been, an illegal restraint of trade. Naturally, Davis noted, the Telephone Group could not engage in any unlawful conduct, as any illegal aspects of the patent pool were void. In addition, he stated other perfectly legal sections of the contracts were still binding, and consequently, the balance of the cross-licensing agreements was still in effect. The Telephone Group could continue to use all patents. The two factions had reached a seemingly insurmountable stalemate. Now, with the very real threat of a government antitrust suit looming ominously over them if their deliberations became public, even more intense, confidential negotiations between the two groups began in earnest. These talks ultimately resulted in formation of NBC and its advisory council in 1926.[15]

Even though discussions about a national network date to 1921, the first successful coast-to-coast system was a temporary network, set up in 1924 to cover the Democratic and Republican national conventions and presidential election. By that summer, 525 stations were broadcasting, and politicians were eager to use this new way of reaching voters.[16] This system developed in late 1923 because AT&T realized the public was exceedingly interested in hearing the national political conventions. Consequently, it decided to provide coverage through experimenting with "chaining stations together," or networking broadcast facilities. In early 1924 the company began negotiating with both major parties for rights to broadcast their respective conventions.[17]

Sensing a way to make money, both political parties haggled with broadcasters, including RCA, AT&T, and individual stations, over monies they would charge anyone for broadcast rights. Broadcasters ultimately balked at the Republican and Democratic national committees' proposals and threatened to abandon plans for coverage. Eventually, Owen Young and others persuaded leaders of the political parties to allow broadcasters to cover the conventions as a public service. Young reasoned that American citizens were eager to hear the conventions for the first time in history and surmised the public would be furious if coverage were excluded. Setting precedent that is still followed today, Young told the national committees that broadcasters would carry the proceedings in the public interest and, most important for the committees, at no cost to the political parties. At the same time, the broadcasters would be able to experiment with networking capabilities.[18]

One year later, with the breakdown of the 1920 patent pooling agreement, the Radio and Telephone groups' intense negotiations formed a national network, with each group getting an exclusive piece of the broadcast pie. The Radio Group would stay in broadcasting, have the rights to manufacture sets and transmitters, and would buy the Telephone Group's broadcast assets. The Telephone Group would remove itself from all broadcast endeavors except to provide interconnection for the Radio Group's networks. As a result of this agreement, each party would make money from its exclusive contribution to network broadcasting. Understandably, members of Congress and the public, as well as other broadcasters, brought accusations of monopoly when the formation of NBC was announced in the summer of 1926.[19]

Both the Radio Group and the Telephone Group had anticipated these accusations. As talks leading to NBC proceeded in the spring and summer of 1926, David Sarnoff of the Radio Group approached Isroy Norr of the public relations firm Ames and Norr and asked him to investigate public reaction to the formation of a broadcast network. Norr responded that accusations of monopoly would undoubtedly arise and to deflect these allegations the new network should form an advisory board to counsel it on matters regarding programming, monopoly, and censorship. This report, presented in more detail in the next chapter, was the beginning of the NBC Advisory Council. Subsequent chapters detail the council's influence over the next two decades on NBC's programming and related matters, especially charges of program censorship.[20]

Program Evolution through 1945

During the Advisory Council's existence, radio programming grew from amateur productions to sophisticated, highly produced performances. The formats that evolved by 1945 included forms familiar to today's audiences, including dramas, documentaries, situation comedies, game shows, news and public affairs programs, sports programming, religious programs, children's shows, and other programs targeting specific audiences. Listener tastes and values, as well as technological developments, helped dictate what American radio broadcasters produced. By the mid-1920s, program types included musical variety shows, concert music, and talks. Some stations experimented with one-act stage plays and presented an early type of variety show, using studio orchestras and vaudeville acts that were playing at local theaters. These shows were completely unrehearsed. Stations also relied heavily on amateurs, who wanted the publicity radio offered.

In 1927 radio entered a seven-year period of unprecedented development of new program types. Dramatic programs, using scripts prepared especially for radio, appeared. Prestige drama, carried for its recognized quality and authorship; informative drama, mostly based on historical incidents; and more popular thrillers and homespun plays attracted audiences. In 1929 an early form of comedy-variety appeared. A series of four or five single comedy acts filled a half-hour period. Song-and-patter teams, such as the Happiness Boys, were very popular on networks and local stations. Begun as a local production in Chicago, the legendary *Amos 'n' Andy* program began as a comedy-patter team and did not adopt a continuing storyline until 1930. By 1930 many evening network-sponsored shows were an hour long, and the most popular network programs were musical variety and concert music.[21]

Program syndication and repetitive patterns for program presentation became the answers to insatiable listener demand. The need for program sharing and recordings became clear, and programming soon evolved formats that lent themselves to repetition. These formats often adapted to the cycle of social activities of 1920s and 1930s households. For example, daytime programming aimed at homemakers evolved, while programs aimed at farmers and their families—nearly half of the U.S. population in the 1920s and 1930s—aired over the noon hour, when farmers came in for their midday meals. Evening programs appealed to general audiences and were presented weekly, with the same basic components being used each week. Permanent cast members and program hosts, as well as recurring storylines or musical types, became key ingredients in these programs.[22]

Between 1930 and 1935 network competition, program sponsorship, and network advertising fostered many of these changes. Sponsors poured money into the new formats, including regular variety (programs that featured a diversity of performers and material), comedy variety (programs built around a featured comedian), "hillbilly" variety (programs that featured country music and acts), human interest programs (usually interview and advice), amateur contests, straight news programs, dramatized news programs (such as *March of Time*), women's daytime serial dramas (better known today as "soap operas"), and later afternoon children's adventure shows.

The early 1930s also saw the evolution of "strip programming," or the scheduling of shows Monday through Friday at the same time, with the introduction of daytime soap operas in 1932. Before then, daytime programs had been scheduled much like that in prime time—once a week, with thirty-minute shows being the most popular. Newscasts were, at most, fifteen-minute "rip and read" presentations with material lifted from local newspaper or national news service reports. To make money as the Depression deepened, local stations introduced commercial religious programs and a "per inquiry" selling technique wherein the station received a portion of the sale for each order mailed to the station.[23]

Programming of the late 1920s and 1930s also saw adaptation of existing media forms to radio. Producers and writers took products of other media and assimilated them. At first, radio reproduced stage, screen, pulpit, and concert hall performances literally. The first radio dramas, for example, were unembellished broadcasts of stage performances done on site or read into a studio microphone with few, if any, changes or sound effects. Soon, producers realized that plays on radio were more effective if they relied on radio's unique qualities. With carefully coordinated music and sound effects performed under controlled studio conditions, adaptations and original plays capitalized on radio's potential for intimacy and became powerful interpretations of an existing form with the audience's imagination supplying the stage's visual element.[24]

From 1935 to 1941, at least six new program forms appeared on radio. While news commentaries and reports had begun in the late 1920s, they did not become a regular program format until Hitler gained power in Europe and Japanese imperialism engulfed the Far East. Quiz programs with audience participants developed in 1936. Panel quiz programs, where several experts appeared as part of a team or jury, and comedy–audience participation programs, such as *Truth or Consequences*, soon followed.

Crime dramas emphasized that "crime does not pay" and capitalized on evening audiences, while telephone giveaway programs allowed the listening audience to participate. Network news increased but found few sponsors during this period. Most stations scheduled at least one daily or weekly "man-on-the-street" program, and by America's entry into World War II in December 1941, recorded music began replacing live musical programs.[25]

From the mid-1930s until the end of World War II, radio prospered. Advertising, network operations, and government regulation evolved into a clearly linked configuration. During the 1920s government regulation under the Radio Act of 1912 collapsed, but passage of the Radio Act of 1927 aimed specifically at broadcasting began to clear the airwaves. By the time its successor, the Communications Act of 1934, was passed and the Federal Communications Commission (FCC) was formed, the Federal Radio Commission (FRC) had cleared up technical problems of the late 1920s and had attacked and eliminated questionable programs or practices, including personal attacks, disreputable medical advice, over-the-air astrological and fortune-telling recommendations, and the like. The FRC abolished stations that carried such programming, actions the courts upheld.[26]

As advertising became the financial underpinning for broadcasting in the late 1920s, broadcasts were divided into two basic types, sponsored and sustaining programs. Sponsored programs were either supplied in their entirety by advertisers or were "participations" in which stations or networks supplied programs with costs for time and talent shared by several advertisers in return for "participating" spot, or commercial, announcements. Traditionally, these programs were fifteen, thirty, or sixty minutes long with a thirty-second station break at the end of the time segment. Station announcements occurred during these breaks and could be either commercial or noncommercial. Sustaining programs were those shows developed and aired by the networks or stations themselves and for which the broadcaster received no revenue. Often, these shows either were in search of a sponsor or were carried primarily for their prestige or goodwill value to the broadcaster. Stations and networks often considered sustaining programs as part of a balanced or well-rounded program service.[27]

No new program formats appeared on the networks from 1941 to 1945, but World War II brought a tremendous increase in local and network newscasts, news commentary, and news analysis. After 1944, when the country suffered from "war weariness," networks programmed a growing number of "escape" programs. Comedy-variety shows grew in popularity, and the number of thriller dramas soared. Prestige programs, such as symphonic concerts, operas, documentaries, dramatic programs, and public affairs broadcasts, increased during the war years. Networks and stations used these programs as public relations tools and to offset heavy taxes on corporate profits, which were set as high as 90 percent. The number of cultural programs also expanded as nonbroadcast companies invested in goodwill public relations efforts and developed programs to offset their tax liabilities. Programs that featured servicemen chosen from the audience were also widely used, both locally and on the networks.[28] Thus, by the end of World War II, program types familiar in electronic media today existed in wide variety.

This world, then, was the environment in which the NBC Advisory Council was formed in 1926 and operated during the next two decades. The council's first members were selected to reflect the major cultural and social concerns and the communal dynamics of the interwar years. Over the next two decades the council greatly influenced program policy and programming development, especially two specific, popular interwar programs, the *National Farm and Home Hour* and the *Music Appreciation Hour*. The former, aimed at rural audiences, relied on resources of both NBC and the U.S. Department of Agriculture, while the latter evolved as the personal project of council member Walter Damrosch, retired conductor of the New York Symphony.

The council's policy pronouncements greatly influenced all broadcasters' carriage of religious programming, programs about controversial issues (especially birth control), and political broadcast policies adopted for both sponsored and sustaining programs, as well as presentation of national defense issues prominent in the late 1930s and through World War II. After Pearl Harbor, the council did not meet formally and was quietly disbanded in 1945 as redundant to the FCC, but until then, the NBC Advisory Council contributed much to early radio development and broadcast policies, many of which lasted well into the 1980s, with several still relevant today.

An Advisory Council Is Formed

WHEN FORMING ADVISORY COUNCILS, corporations select members whose ethics, morals, value systems, beliefs, articles of faith, and attitudes are not acutely out of step with contemporary societal and business norms. They seek highly qualified, experienced, mature, sophisticated members who collectively know societal dynamics, as well as the cultural and competitive environments facing the corporation.[1] As Robert Mueller notes in his book *The Director's and Officer's Guide to Advisory Boards*, "Like the medieval privy councils, a modern advisory board may be modeled as a private, confidential council, or may have a publicly identified organizational identity."[2] NBC's council was definitely the latter, as its decrees and pronouncements were readily distributed to the press.

During its nearly two decades of existence, the NBC Advisory Council acted to curb undesirable speech over radio, and its statements reflected the conservative sentiments found in society as a whole. Lasting until the mid-1940s, when it was disbanded as a redundancy to FCC oversight, the council heard few complaints, but those few protests were about issues vital to free speech on network radio. To understand the council's proclamations better, an overview of the formation and initial membership of the council is warranted.

Plans for a National Broadcast Company Emerge

Concerns in the mid-1920s over the creation of a national radio network led to the advisory council's formation. When a network was first proposed in

1921, RCA's board of directors set up a special committee to investigate the concept. That committee issued a report calling for a limited network of stations located at suitable points throughout the United States, but the full board adopted a wait-and-see attitude. Four years later, RCA and others were actively discussing formation of a network structure.[3] Some industry leaders, such as H. P. Davis of Westinghouse, recognized that small stations and high-power stations could coexist in such a design. Smaller stations would serve their specific locales, while superpower stations would serve both regional and national audiences. Davis also noted that programs supplied by these stations should not be subjected to formal state or federal censorship, because it would stifle industry initiative. Rather, "public opinion," as discerned by broadcasters, should dictate programming.[4]

The RCA Committee on Broadcasting—David Sarnoff, H. P. Davis, and Albert Davis—took this perspective into account, and in January 1926 they issued a report on chain broadcasting to the RCA board of directors. That report stated that GE, RCA, and Westinghouse stations should develop a new network to provide quality programming to national audiences, but added that no station would lose its identity under the plan, as each would maintain a local service. The network plan would maintain and encourage both services through contracts that specified times for national programs.[5] On January 22, 1926, RCA's board of directors adopted the committee's recommendation, and the national network–local outlet structure of American broadcasting was conceived.[6]

As plans advanced for what would become the National Broadcasting Company, some individuals, notably Martin Rice of RCA and H. P. Davis of Westinghouse, warned that independent broadcasters and some government officials perceived the growing possibility of monopoly and censorship by RCA, GE, and Westinghouse, who shared control of the network. Official RCA policy did not reflect these concerns, though, until a public relations firm hired by RCA to look into public reaction to a network's formation suggested RCA needed to head off potential charges as mentioned in chapter 1, in July 1926. RCA commercial manager David Sarnoff contacted Isroy M. Norr to study public perceptions about the proposed broadcast company.[7]

Norr submitted a fifteen-page confidential report to Sarnoff, who sent it to Harbord and Owen Young, chief executive officer of both RCA and GE. The report began with the admonition that "to minimize the cry of 'monopoly' which is likely to greet the announcement of the broadcasting plans contemplated by the R.C.A. group," certain accommodating policies should be established and announced to the general public. Among those policies was the establishment of an advisory council.[8]

Norr suggested the council include members of all facets of American society, so that the new broadcast company would "have the cooperation of distinguished leaders in American public life."[9] While deflecting cries of monopoly was paramount, the council's additional mission was threefold: (1) to reflect broadcasting from a public standpoint; (2) to obtain cooperation from educational and musical enterprises for sustaining broadcast programs; and (3) to secure public support for policies the Broadcasting Service Company of America may need to undertake. Norr emphasized that to further deflate charges of monopoly, RCA should also adopt a policy of local autonomy for stations that affiliated themselves with the new national service.[10]

Sarnoff pushed adoption of Norr's suggestions, as both men recognized such councils had become a growing part of business decision making in the twentieth century. While advisory bodies dated to English monarchs' privy councils, their corporate descendants often tapped into external factors relevant to the corporations' needs. In this case, an advisory body to NBC could assist with decision making and help shape corporate policy regarding programming. The proposed council would be an invaluable resource in advising NBC on matters of importance by interpreting information and facts from additional perspectives. Both men also knew that council members could legitimize company actions if they selected well-recognized people who were influential, prominent, and respected within society.[11]

Critical to RCA's acceptance and formation of a council were announcements appearing one week later in the New York City papers that RCA and AT&T were developing a nationwide broadcast system. As Norr predicted, several newspapers alleged monopoly and censorship.[12] On July 22, the New York *Tribune* page-one headline read, "WEAF Sold; Air Combine Is Forecast." The paper charged that the sale of broadcasting station WEAF to RCA was the first step of RCA, GE, and Westinghouse "to acquire a practical monopoly of the air, through control of the important broadcasting stations."[13] The New York *World* wrote the next day that RCA planned to extend WEAF's chain of stations and that AT&T would supply wires for interconnections. Two New York *World* articles, headlined "Coming Monopoly of Broadcasting by WEAF Is Seen" and "WEAF Sale Only Part of Huge Deal," complained that independent stations would be hampered if they attempted to set up a rival network, because interconnecting lines and competing programs would be difficult to procure.[14] Press reports stressed that AT&T and RCA could dominate broadcasting under the arrangements. Clearly after these articles appeared, the new network needed to combat perceptions of possible censorship, and plans for a national company with an advisory council moved forward rapidly.

Consequently, among the suggestions highlighted in the proposal sent to the RCA board of directors on August 10 was that an advisory council function as "a court of appeal on matters of policy on programs and entertainment, as distinguished from business administration, and in cases of alleged discrimination." The council would also advise executives and suggest rules, which the company could adopt, dealing with questions of fairness in the use of facilities.[15] In addition to the council, the recommendations to the board outlined the business, financial, engineering, and production aspects of the new company. RCA's board readily adopted the recommendations.

An Advisory Council Is Formed

Interoffice memos between Young and NBC's newly appointed president, Merlin Aylesworth, show a genuine interest in creating a council as "a very helpful and constructive agency," one that "would be much more useful than . . . a buffer against fault finders" or a "decorative body of names." Young wanted this "constructive agency" to meet regularly and to be "a real committee of advice as to how we can make this radio broadcasting of the greatest service to the public, and how, on the other hand, we can avoid its misuse."[16] The council would consist of twelve to fifteen members. As Young began selecting potential candidates, he looked for well-rounded, peer-respected individuals who could be trusted to preserve confidentiality.

As histories of advisory councils in the early twentieth century show, Young's actions were in sync with the formation of other contemporary consultative bodies. Advisory council members for any organization had to be recognized for their wisdom, as well as the educational, career, and cultural experiences they could bring to the decision-making process. Accordingly, on most councils, members generally were older than forty-five, as younger people had not established themselves sufficiently in their fields. When selecting council members, companies also tried to include a variety of viewpoints or perspectives they believed important to their operation. While councils were set up to reflect various shades of opinion or to represent various interests, companies also desired consensus and collegiality in decision making.[17]

Council advisers and company officers had to be collegial and have mutual esteem, as council members often became "insiders" with regard to business operations. Then, just as today, such councils served as focus groups or sounding boards for proposed or existing company policies and provided viewpoints on matters likely to have an impact on the corporation and its policies. In general, advisory councils functioned as "creatures of the board or top management," and members concerned themselves with overall corporate policies and guidelines that promoted the business. They provided boards with "special peer-acceptable insight" into various situations facing the corporation. Therefore, in forming councils, companies selected members to represent certain constituencies, different geographical locales, or different ideological perspectives. But these individuals needed to see beyond their own parochial interests and had to relate well with the world around them. So, while representative membership was a planned, not chance, occurrence, members' value systems, beliefs, and attitudes usually were not exceedingly out of step with contemporary societal or business norms.[18]

The initial list of potential NBC Advisory Council appointees vividly illustrated this fact, as the selected individuals reflected the dominant social and political components of 1920s America. Management and labor were represented, as were business and farm concerns. Government officials, especially from military backgrounds, joined representatives from geographically different sections of the country and spokesmen from cultural concerns such as the Metropolitan Opera and symphonic groups. Three members represented the dominant Judeo-Christian beliefs—one representative each from the Catholic Church, the Federal Council of Churches in America (Protestant), and the Jewish faith.[19] Later, the Broadcast Committee added the Federation of American Women's Clubs to represent women's interests, and with this amendment the general makeup of the council was established and approved.[20]

The Council's Composition

The list of final Advisory Council invitees was drawn up in a meeting held in Young's office October 28, 1926. Selected by Merlin Aylesworth and Owen Young, people who reflected various facets of American life received invitations to join the council. Replies came back quickly, and the first Advisory Council was formed and formally announced by Aylesworth during NBC's inauguration ceremonies in November 1926.[21] When RCA publicly announced plans for the Advisory Council, *Literary Digest*, a major publication of the day, heralded it as a positive step toward the elimination of discrimination. The editors of the noted magazine wrote, "The general plan [for NBC] calls for the financing of a network of stations that will give a nationwide service, with improved programs supervised by an advisory council of twelve representatives of various shades of public opinion."[22]

Among the eminent individuals selected were three prominent jurists and statesmen: John W. Davis, Charles Evans Hughes, and Elihu Root. Their relevance to council appointment is seen in their respective biographies, and these as well as the other council members' accomplishments are worth noting here, as they illustrate the individuals' importance to society in the 1920s and therefore their significance in being appointed to the Advisory Council.[23] Each man also reflected certain political stances relevant in the 1920s—Davis was a Democrat, while Hughes and Root were Republicans.

John William Davis, born April 13, 1873, in Clarksburg, West Virginia, served from 1911 through 1913 as a representative from West Virginia in Congress, where he was one of the coauthors of the Clayton Anti-Trust Act. After serving in Congress, Davis was U.S. solicitor general from 1913 to 1918 and the American ambassador to Great Britain from 1918 to 1921. After 1921 he practiced law in New York City and became regarded by many as the most distinguished constitutional attorney of his time. Over the years he argued 140 cases before the Supreme Court, and today is probably best known as defending South Carolina's school segregation laws before the Supreme Court in 1954 in the collection of cases known as *Brown v. Board of Education*. In 1924 he became the Democratic nominee for president, when on the Democratic Convention's 103rd ballot, he was selected as a compromise candidate between the deadlocked proponents of Alfred E. Smith and William Gibbs McAdoo. He lost to Calvin Coolidge. He died March 24, 1955.

Charles Evans Hughes was born in Glen Falls, New York, on April 11, 1862. He attended college at both Colgate and Brown Universities and graduated from the latter in 1881. Three years later he received his law degree from Columbia University. He came to national attention in 1905 when he served as counsel to the New York state legislature, which was investigating insurance business operations and the gas industry. Perceived as fair and thorough in his investigations and exposure of these major scandals, Hughes was elected New York's governor in 1906 and reelected in 1908. While he faced much organized opposition for his reforms, he succeeded in setting up two public service commissions and began reorganization of state government. In 1910 President Taft appointed him an associate justice of the U.S. Supreme Court. He resigned in 1916 to run for the presidency on the Republican ticket and lost the election by a small margin to Woodrow Wilson. He served as secretary of state from 1921 to 1925 and directed the 1921 Washington Naval Conference for arms limitations. He initiated the Dawes Plan, a reconstruction plan for Germany to relieve it from its crushing World War I debts. In 1928 he led the American delegation to the Pan American Peace Conference and became a judge of the World Court. He resigned in 1930 when he became the eleventh chief justice of the Supreme Court, a position he held until 1941. During the New Deal, Hughes fought vigorously against President Roosevelt's attempt to "pack" the court in 1937, and many historians consider him the greatest influence in defeating FDR's court reorganization bill. He died August 27, 1948, in Washington, D.C.

Elihu Root at age seventy-seven was by far the oldest person appointed to the Advisory Council. Root was born in Clinton, New York, on February 15, 1845, and was admitted to the bar in 1867. He attended Hamilton College, where his father was a professor, and studied law at New York University. He started practicing law in New York City and gained fame in 1873 as counsel for William "Boss" Tweed, who was charged with political corruption. At the same time, Root became prominent in Republican politics and was appointed U.S. attorney of the southern district of New York in 1883. Two years later he returned to private practice and became well known as a corporate lawyer. In 1899 President William McKinley appointed him secretary of war. As secretary, he planned the Army War College, introduced the principle of the General Staff, and greatly improved the efficiency of the War Department. In 1905 he became President Theodore Roosevelt's secretary of state, a post he held until 1909, when the New York legislature elected him to the U.S. Senate. (At that time, voters did not directly elect U.S. senators.) For his tireless efforts to ensure international peace, Root won the 1912 Nobel peace prize. Even though he was a critic of the League of Nations, he helped plan the Permanent Court of International Justice, better known as the World Court, which the League sponsored. He died February 7, 1937, just a few days shy of his ninety-second birthday.

As prominent jurists these three men often led discussion as policy was formed in the council's early years. Collectively, they were concerned with radio's impact on society, and fairness in access to and use of the medium was important to all of them. But they also recognized radio's unique dynamic in reaching millions instantaneously. Because radio came into the home and could do so without regard to who was listening, these men thought radio needed to be treated differently from the print media.

In addition to recognizing the contributions of these men's legal and political backgrounds to the council, Owen Young and Merlin Aylesworth knew that religious concerns held overt, dominant positions in the cultural and social milieu of the 1920s. Those holding religious positions greatly influenced decision making in many spheres, including media. So Young and Aylesworth selected three men to represent what they considered the dominant American religious denominations—Jewish, Catholic, and Protestant. They chose Julius Rosenwald, president of Sears, Roebuck, and Company, to represent Jews; Morgan J. O'Brien, attorney from New York, to advocate for Catholics; and Rev. Charles F. MacFarland, General

Secretary, Federal Council of the Churches of Christ in America, to speak for Protestants. These three men were largely responsible for developing policies NBC followed for decades in its coverage of religious issues and contentious topics having religious implications, such as birth control and improper sexual innuendo.

Julius Rosenwald was born August 12, 1862, and educated in the public school systems in Springfield, Illinois. In 1895 he joined Sears, Roebuck, and Company and was its president from 1910 until 1925. In 1916 President Wilson appointed him to the Advisory Commission of the Council of National Defense as chairman of its committee on supplies. In 1917 he established the Julius Rosenwald Fund. As he thoroughly disliked perpetual funds, he mandated all monies be spent within twenty-five years of his death, which came on January 6, 1932. By 1948 the fund had donated more than $22.5 million to various causes, primarily establishing medical services for low-income blacks and developing over five thousand rural public schools for blacks in the South. These schools had the capacity for 567,000 students. His many other philanthropies included Jewish relief in the Middle East and Russia, grants to educational institutions, and funds for twenty-five YMCA and three YWCA buildings in cities with large black populations. His gift of $3 million helped establish the Museum of Science and Industry in Chicago. Overall, he contributed about $63 million over his lifetime and in the twenty-five years after his death.

Attorney and former New York supreme court judge Morgan O'Brien was born April 28, 1852, in New York City. He graduated from St. John's College in 1873 and received a master's degree from St. Francis Xavier College in 1873 and a law degree from Columbia in 1904. O'Brien was elected to New York's supreme court in 1887 and served until 1915. He then joined the law firm of Conboy, Hewitt, O'Brien, and Boardman and was a trustee of the Provident Loan Society of New York. He received the Chevalier Legion of Honor from France. O'Brien died June 16, 1937.

Born December 12, 1866, in Boston, Charles MacFarland represented the Protestant denominations on the Advisory Council. From 1885 to 1892 MacFarland was general manager of T. O. Gardener & Company, Manufacturers. He received his bachelor's degree from Yale in 1897 and was ordained a Congregational minister later that year. Two years later he received his Ph.D. from Yale. From 1900 to 1911 he was a minister to several congregations in Massachusetts and Connecticut. In 1911 he became social services secretary of the Federated Council of the Churches of Christ in America and was appointed its general secretary in 1912, a post he held until 1931. He died October 26, 1956.

While Rosenwald, Morgan, and MacFarland enhanced the council's religious diversity, Young and Aylesworth knew the council also needed to advance the nation's geographic and educational mix as well. They chose Edwin Alderman, president of the University of Virginia, Francis D. Farrell, president of Kansas Agricultural College, and Henry M. Robinson, president of the First National Bank of Los Angeles, for their educational and regional backgrounds and accomplishments.

Edwin Alderman was born in Wilmington, North Carolina, on May 15, 1861. In 1882 he graduated from the University of North Carolina, and in 1896 he received his D.C.L. from the University of the South. Professorships of history at North Carolina State Normal College in 1892, and of education at the University of North Carolina one year later, followed. University presidencies came in quick succession: UNC in 1896, Tulane University four years later, and the University of Virginia in 1904. He held the last position until his death on April 29, 1931. Alderman could claim, among other honors, chief editorship of the Library of Southern Literature and authorship of several books, including *Southern Idealism*, *The Spirit of the South*, *Sectionalism and Nationality*, and *The Growing South*.

Born in Smithfield, Utah, on March 13, 1883, Francis Farrell was one of the younger members of the council. He graduated from Utah State College in 1907 and soon joined the U.S. Department of Agriculture as a scientific assistant in the investigations of cereals, serving from 1907 to 1910. From then until 1918, he worked at various universities and at USDA research sites, finally becoming dean of the division of agriculture and director of the USDA Agricultural Experiment Station at Kansas State University. In 1925 he became president of Kansas State, a position he held until his retirement in 1943. He was the author of numerous articles and papers on agriculture and education. He died February 13, 1976.

Henry Robinson was born in Ravenna, Ohio, on September 12, 1868. He attended Cornell University for two years and practiced law in Ohio and New York from 1890 to 1905. In 1906 he and his family moved to California to join the Security–First National Bank in Los Angeles. He was with the Council of National Defense in 1917 and 1918 and was a member of the Supreme Economic Council of the Paris Peace Council in 1919. In 1924 he was a member of the committee that proposed the Dawes Plan for Germany's reconstruction. He was a trustee of the Huntington Library and Art Gallery, the California Institute of Technology, and the Hispanic Society of America. He died November 3, 1937.

The balance of the council represented various other constituencies important in the 1920s. Radio's use for cultural and social enhancement was represented by Walter Damrosch, conductor of the New York Symphony Orchestra, and Dr. Henry S. Pritchett, president of the Carnegie Foundation. Promoting labor interests was William Green, president of the American Federation of Labor, while management had two advocates—Dwight W. Morrow, financier with the J. P. Morgan Company, and Guy Tripp, chairman of the board of Westinghouse. Mrs. Mary Sherman, president of the General Federation of Women's Clubs of America, was the last person Young and Aylesworth chose for the council; she would represent women's issues. Each of these individuals brought a range of experiences and stellar credentials to the council.

Born on January 30, 1862, in Breslau, Prussia, Walter Damrosch immigrated to the United States in 1871 with his father, Leopold, noted violinist and conductor. Leopold founded the New York Symphony Society in 1878 and conducted its orchestra. Walter succeeded his father as director of the society, which he reorganized in 1903, and served as its symphony's conductor until 1927. In 1925 he conducted the New York Symphony in its first radio broadcast, so he was a natural choice as a member who would represent music and cultural activities on the NBC Advisory Council. In 1928 Damrosch became NBC's "music counsel," and for the next two decades he worked tirelessly to educate the population, especially children, about serious music. Many schoolchildren heard his *Music Appreciation Hour,* which aired from 1928 to 1942, and came to value composers such as Wagner, Gershwin, Stravinsky, and Ravel. In addition to his conducting and educational work, Damrosch also composed operas such as *Cyrano de Bergerac* in 1913 and *The Man without a Country* in 1937. He died December 22, 1950.

Born April 16, 1857, in Fayette, Missouri, Henry Pritchett graduated in 1875 from Pritchett College, organized in 1866 by his father in Glasgow, Missouri. Pritchett became an astronomer, like his father, and pursued further education, finally receiving his Ph.D. in Munich in 1894. Before that, however, he worked in various capacities as an astronomer, finally taking the position of professor of astronomy and director of the observatory at Washington University in St. Louis in 1883. From 1900 to 1906 he was the president of the Massachusetts Institute of Technology. In 1906 Pritchett became president of the Carnegie Foundation for the Advancement of Teaching. In 1930 he was named president emeritus of the foundation. He died August 28, 1939.

William Green was an American labor leader and president of the American Federation of Labor (AFL) from 1924 through 1952. Born in Coshocton, Ohio, on March 3, 1870, Green rose through the ranks of the United Mine Workers of America, serving as its secretary-treasurer from 1912 to 1924. With backing from John L. Lewis, Green was elected president of the AFL to succeed Samuel Gompers. He gradually built the organization's membership, but in 1935 eight of the largest unions split away under the leadership of John Lewis to form the Committee for Industrial Organization (CIO), which organized workers in industrial unions. Green then led the AFL in a subsequent struggle with the CIO. In 1939 he published *Labor and Democracy*, which set forth his philosophy of labor and management. After Green's death on November 21, 1952, George Meany became president of the AFL.

Dwight Morrow was an American lawyer, banker, and diplomat. Morrow was born in Huntington, West Virginia, on January 11, 1873. He practiced law in New York City and in 1914 began working for the banking house of J. P. Morgan and Company. After the United States became involved in World War I, he was a chief civilian aide to General John J. Pershing, and his outstanding work on the Military Board of Supply earned him the Distinguished Service Medal. As tensions between Mexico and the United States intensified in the mid-1920s, Morrow became President Coolidge's ambassador to Mexico from 1927 to 1930. He helped alleviate the ill feeling aroused by the Mexican government's expropriation of U.S. holdings in Mexico, and his service marked a new spirit of cooperation in U.S. relations with Latin America. In 1929 his daughter, Anne Spencer Morrow, married one of the heroes of the 1920s, aviator Charles Lindbergh. Murrow died October 5, 1931.

Born in Wells, Maine, on April 22, 1865, Guy Tripp received a basic education at South Berwick Academy and then moved into business. During his illustrious business career he held positions at various national and international companies, including American Sugar Refining Company, Brazilian Securities Corporation, Canadian Westinghouse Co., Ltd., and Chase National Bank. The balance of his career was with Westinghouse. In January 1918 he was appointed the chief of the production division of the Department of Ordnance and received the Distinguished Service Medal "for exceptionally meritorious service to the United States Government" in 1919. He passed away on June 14, 1927, a few months after the first Advisory Council meeting.

Mary Belle King Sherman was born in Albion, New York, in 1862 to the Rufus King family. She was educated in public schools in Rochester, New York, and at the Park Institute in Chicago. In 1887 she married John Dickenson Sherman, a Chicago newspaperman and editor. They had one child, John King Sherman. She taught at John Marshall Law School in Chicago and wrote *Parliamentary Law and Rules of Procedure*. She became secretary of the Chicago Women's Clubs and, from 1924 to 1928, served as president of the General Federation of Women's Clubs. During World War I she was a member of the National War Gardens Commission and an assistant to the director of the school garden army of the Federal Bureau of Education. She also served as "the woman commissioner" on the George Washington Bicentennial Celebration committee in 1922. An avid conservationist, Sherman was a trustee of the National Park Association and was active in the establishment of the Rocky Mountain National Park. She was also active in securing recognition of "home-maker" as an occupation in the 1930 census. She died at her home in Denver on January 15, 1935, from injuries suffered in an auto accident in Washington, D.C., several months earlier.

In an attempt to round out the council and to include several governmental representatives, Young had also invited representatives of the Army and Navy to participate as formal council members because, in the event of war, he expected RCA to place its facilities at the disposal of military in the name of national defense. "From that standpoint," he wrote General Charles Summerall, Army chief of staff, and Admiral E. W. Eberle, chief of naval operations, "it is important that these officers might serve on the advisory council in peace time and thereby acquire some knowledge of the facilities themselves." But both men declined, citing regulations prohibiting military personnel from being actively identified with commercial enterprises, such as NBC.[24]

In the letters of invitation Young wrote to each council member mentioned above, he echoed his perception of the council's public service mission, which he had emphasized in his interoffice correspondence. He underscored his genuine belief that NBC's selection of national programs carried with it a corresponding responsibility that could more wisely be exercised with the advice of "a disinterested and impartial body of American citizens representing widely different interests." Young added "while a Democracy [sic] is learning to handle an instrument of such power (as radio), it is most important that the decisions of its executives relating to broadcasting programs and public service should be subject to review and correction by an Advisory Council."[25]

Replies came quickly. In his letter of acceptance University of Virginia president Edwin Alderman told Young it seemed to him to be perfectly clear that a free radio was as important to the liberties of the people as a free press,[26] while Morgan O'Brien complimented Young on his highly regarded international reputation, adding "nothing could be more agreeable to me than to work with, or under you, in one of your many useful and patriotic endeavors."[27]

When prospective members accepted Young's invitation, he wrote to thank them and to reiterate his vision of the council. "It will act as a restraint on the broadcasting organization and will tend to make them consider carefully all questions affecting the use of their facilities," and then he added, "It will likewise be a restraint upon the foolish complaints from people who, without any consideration at all, just assume they may be discriminated against." Finally, he said the council would give the public at large the feeling that they have a right to go to a competent and impartial body regarding the misuse of the facilities. According to Young, the preservation of this right of appeal was perhaps more important than the council's ability to make programming suggestions.[28]

The council's makeup was announced on NBC's inaugural program on November 15, 1926, in what Young and Aylesworth called "the most prestigious broadcasting program ever presented." The program brought enthusiastic responses from all over the United States, with approximately 140,000 complimentary letters and telegrams being received.[29] In early December, NBC's board of directors formally approved the council,[30] and the members held their first meeting on February 18, 1927—just five days before President Coolidge signed the Radio Act.

The Council's First Meeting

In preparation for this meeting, Young recognized what others had also observed: that advisory councils were most effective when the advisee decided what subjects to put on the agenda and informed the advisers well in advance of the council meeting. Using such an approach allowed board members to form their own opinions, informally and independently, with minimal preparation other than thinking about the issues on the agenda.[31] Of course, members could bring their own concerns to the meetings, and they sometimes did, as subsequent chapters will show. The agenda for this meeting was brief and consisted largely of time for members to become better acquainted with each other and the NBC executive hierarchy.

At this meeting Young introduced NBC's officers, explained the circumstances leading to NBC's formation, and noted NBC's purpose "is to provide the best programs available for broadcasting in the United States and to secure their distribution over the widest possible area." He added, "The wise guidance of able men of diversified experience located in different parts of the country is sought in order that the facilities of the National Broadcasting Company may be put to their best possible use in the public interest, which is the only way to serve the business interests of the founders of the plan."[32] Later he stated his vision for the council:

[We] hope the Advisory Council may be considered as a court of appeal for complaints. There will be less complaints [*sic*] because of its existence. I should expect few will ever come to your attention unless they are really serious and difficult cases. In that case, they should be decided in the public interest. But the fact that you exist means that the National Broadcasting Company's organization itself will be most careful to avoid unfair discrimination or misuse knowing that an appeal lies over [them].
. . . The fact of your existence for the purposes indicated is undoubtedly of more importance than the work you will have to do in this particular field. To my mind, your most important service will be in the way of constructive suggestion as to how we can enlarge and improve broadcasting service from time to time.[33]

Thus the first meeting of the council was largely organizational, and discussion focused on hopes for the council to be a viable contributor to network program decisions. Young noted that six areas of special interest existed, and he appointed council members as coordinators of committees for programming in these areas: agriculture—Francis Farrell; church activities—Charles MacFarland; education—Edwin Alderman; music and culture—Walter Damrosch; labor—William Green; and women's activities—Mary Sherman.[34] These committees were all "committees of one" with the exception of the church activities committee. Joining MacFarland, who represented Protestants, were Julius Rosenwald and Morgan O'Brien to represent Jews and Catholics, respectively.

These committees were to oversee and to suggest programming in their respective areas. That NBC in general and Young in particular regarded all members as part of a "working" council is evident in the honorarium of one thousand dollars each member received annually for his or her service. This stipend was nearly one-and-one-half times the average per capita income in the mid-1920s, and the amount reflects the significant contributions Young and NBC anticipated the council members would make to the fledgling industry. At this time Young also believed the council would meet frequently during the year to discuss and to evaluate issues related to programs and to hear any complaints regarding NBC's use of the airwaves.[35]

Of course, when the council began, radio programming was in its infancy, but almost twenty years later when it disbanded, radio's so-called golden age was at its zenith. By 1928 NBC had begun full-time coast-to-coast broadcasting on both its networks, the Red and the Blue. With the advent of these networks, as well as CBS's nationwide network, advertisers began to see radio as another means of reaching their audiences. In 1928 network coverage made programs available to 80 percent of American homes, although only 30 percent owned receivers at this time.[36]

As outlined in chapter 1, by the mid-1930s programs could be classified into four broad categories—variety, music, dramatic, and talks—each of which could be further subdivided. Variety, for instance, included vaudeville, amateur and talent shows, hillbilly and country-western programs, and children's variety shows. Music included all live musical forms from concert to contemporary, as recorded music, at least on the networks, was largely forbidden. "Dramatic" programs included thriller-adventure, situation comedies, women's serials (or soap operas), anthology and prestige, and all other scripted forms that were not considered speeches or talks. Talks included speeches, news, public affairs and forums, sports play-by-play, religious programs, and, later in the 1930s, quiz programs. Some programs combined classifications.[37]

But in 1927 these program forms were yet to be developed, and at the council's next meeting in 1928, council members—unlike those of many boards who simply endorsed or ratified company decisions—became instrumental in forming NBC programs and programming policy. During the meeting council members suggested two programs, which NBC developed. One—the *National Farm and Home Hour*—became a staple on NBC radio until the 1950s. The other—the *Music Appreciation Hour*—was a model for educational programs suitable for radio, and it remained on the air until pressure for news coverage in World War II overshadowed it in 1942. The evolution of both is reviewed in the next chapter.

At its 1928 meeting the council also began setting up procedures regarding acceptance and broadcast of religious programs. Over the next year the religious activities subcommittee developed guidelines for accepting religiously oriented programs on the network, policies that aided NBC in its refusal of controversial religious speakers. Other broadcasters and organizations, including the National Association of Broadcasters, followed suit and adopted the same or similar principles for carriage of religious programs. These guidelines are considered in chapter 4.

Sustaining Program Development

THE FARM ECONOMIC CRISES during the interwar years and NBC's desire to reach rural listeners, who comprised more than 40 percent of the potential audience, resulted in the formation of two distinguished, long-running sustaining programs: the *National Farm and Home Hour* and the *Music Appreciation Hour.* These two programs were directly influenced by members of the NBC Advisory Council, and both brought rural audiences news, entertainment, and educational fare that otherwise would not have been available outside major cities. In advancing these programs NBC executives fulfilled what they genuinely saw as one of radio's major obligations—reaching isolated communities with material that truly was a public service.

Rural America in the 1920s and throughout the 1930s suffered tremendous economic hardship. Immediately after World War I, U.S. agriculture flourished. European relief programs provided new markets, and farmers brought more land into cultivation. Because of this prosperity, farmers borrowed heavily to expand operations, but in the summer and fall of 1920 farm markets collapsed and crop prices fell by 50 percent in 1920–21. Causes for this precipitous decline included increased European farm production, changes in diet and fashion in the United States, and cessation of U.S. government loans to European countries for purchase of U.S. farm commodities. By 1925 the need for farm relief was evident.

Relief efforts in the 1920s were unable to restore affluence to American agriculture. Under President Warren Harding's administration new forms of credit and credit institutions attempted to aid farmers with their debt burden but failed. Congress set controls over middlemen such as meat packers and grain merchants who had exploited farmers in the past, but these proved to be ineffective. Harding and his successor, Calvin Coolidge, also tried to set tariffs on imported goods, but these were unsuccessful. In addition, other plans generated to help farmers such as crop diversification, soil conservation, and creation of cooperative marketing associations came to nothing.[1]

At the same time, farm bloc states tried to create a system of government support for the agricultural economy through a system known as "parity." Parity pricing would have set prices for farm goods at levels enabling farmers to purchase given amounts of prewar goods and services. Surplus produce would be sent abroad, with equalization fees assessed farmers to recover losses on any overseas transactions. When Congress passed such bills in the mid to late 1920s, President Coolidge vetoed them.[2] After the 1929 stock market crash, urban woes joined rural troubles. During these early Depression years government policy was aimed at aiding farmers, but the deepening economic emergency and weather-related crop failures intensified the farm crisis. Clearly the agricultural sector languished, and radio's ability to reach remote areas with information to aid farm families and programs to entertain them became a great hope of both government officials and broadcast operators.

Assessing Programming Needs of Rural Audiences

Minutes of the 1928 council meeting show no complaints were filed with the Advisory Council during NBC's first year.[3] Young began this meeting by recognizing a new council member, Paul Cravath, who replaced General Tripp, who died June 14, 1927. Cravath had been born in Berlin Heights, Ohio, on July 14, 1861. He earned his bachelor's and master's degrees from Oberlin in 1882 and 1887, respectively. Between these years he received his law degree in 1886 from Columbia, and in 1923 he earned a doctor of laws degree from the same university. His distinguished legal career included representing the U.S. Treasury and being a member of the Inter-Allied War Conference in Paris. In 1919 for his World War I duties, he received not only the Distinguished Service Medal from General J. J. Pershing but also the French Chevalier Legion of Honor. He also was president of the New York Metropolitan Opera. He died on July 1, 1940.

After Cravath's introduction, the council members reviewed the work of its six subcommittees—agriculture, education, music, labor, religious activities, and women's activities. These reports aided NBC in fleshing out its program schedule as its network expanded in the Midwest and West.

By March 1928 installation of facilities in Chicago enabled NBC to reach most of the central part of the country, while network expansion up and down the West Coast brought programs to listeners there.[4] The agricultural committee, headed by Kansas State College president Francis Farrell, recognized that most farmers and their families had the same general interests in entertainment and information as nonfarm populations. To reach rural populations Farrell encouraged NBC to develop an hour-long program beginning at noon that included weather, market reports, coverage of national laws and proposed legislation affecting agriculture, and musical entertainment by a fifteen-piece orchestra and vocalists. He also suggested NBC carry talks by agricultural experts and features for farm wives and children. Because special coverage of leading agricultural events had been broadcast in 1927 to great success, NBC executives noted many similar programs were planned for 1928. Mary Sherman, representing the subcommittee on women's activities, agreed with Farrell that specific programs needed to be developed for specialized audiences and encouraged development of daytime programs expressly aimed at women. She stressed that NBC should continue its evening program schedule, as both men and women want to enjoy these programs together. To her, this approach encouraged stronger relationships among family members.[5]

The council's education subcommittee endorsed creation of a national service to bring lectures to students around the country. Such a program would be divided into three subcategories: high school or secondary education, college or university education, and adult education. The last of these was the most diverse, of course, and the subcommittee encouraged any program aimed at adults to be less formal than those aimed at the other two groups. Scientific talks, discussions of health and hygiene issues, and current events presentations, including education about political subjects, were three areas targeted for adults. For colleges and universities, talks involving "the best talent on any given subject" could offer students, as well as the broader listening public, a unique opportunity. The same would be true for secondary school students. But no matter what programs evolved, Owen Young suggested avoiding the label "educational" in favor of "feature programs." "Let them be educated in spite of themselves," he noted, referring to listeners.[6]

Labor leader William Green, as head of the committee on labor, congratulated NBC for the wide variety of programs that were "highly appreciated by workers and their families," even though those shows were not specifically aimed at the working class. Green noted workers applauded NBC's "tolerant, broadminded attitude" in "permitting Labor [sic] to use its service and through such service bring Labor's message to the American people." In writing for the committee on music, William Damrosch echoed the labor committee's appreciation for NBC's presentations of both sponsored and sustaining high-quality musical programs of all types, from operas to concertos and secular songs to sacred music. Especially noted were the young people's concerts presented on Saturday nights. These, as well as experiments with programs presented during the school day, were met with great success.[7] Damrosch believed the experimental music programs should be formalized and offered to schools on a weekly basis, and these programs became the basis for the *Music Appreciation Hour.*

Aylesworth noted these suggestions and closed his remarks to the second meeting of the council by reviewing the Davis Amendment to equalize broadcast facilities among various regions of the country. Sponsored by Tennessee representative Ewin Davis and later passed by Congress, the amendment to the Radio Act of 1927 would reallocate broadcast facilities on an equitable basis among five geographic regions of the nation, roughly the Northeast, South, upper and lower Midwest, and the West. Aylesworth stated in any plan Congress needed to consider the distribution of talent available in various parts of the county, as well as the distribution and concentration of the population. He felt assured that Congress would do so[8] but was privately worried about the effect any change would have on broadcasting's growth.

The Farm and Home Hour

After this Advisory Council meeting, Kansas State University president Frank Farrell discussed his idea for a program aimed at farmers and rural audiences with Aylesworth and Frank Mullen, the agriculture program director at NBC's wholly owned and operated station, WMAQ, in Chicago. Farrell acknowledged experimental radio programs aimed at farmers. At first NBC executives and executives at Montgomery Ward wanted to work with the U.S. Department of Agriculture (USDA) to present an experimental program, *The Dinner Bell Hour,* from noon to one central time each afternoon. Montgomery Ward would pay about $250,000 for one year's worth of shows beginning October 2, 1928. By the next June, however, Montgomery Ward no longer wanted to continue the experiment. But because the USDA deemed the program successful in reaching the rural audience and wanted to continue it, NBC decided it would carry the broadcasts on a sustaining basis if it could not find a sponsor.[9]

Thus NBC, with USDA support, inaugurated what would become the *Farm and Home Hour* on July 8, 1929, from NBC Blue stations in Washington, D.C., and Chicago. Initially, the program was forty-five minutes long, with about twenty minutes of economic information and agricultural news, including current weather reports coming from D.C. and the balance, entertainment programming, from Chicago. It ran Monday through Saturday beginning at 12:30 P.M. central time. Saturday's programs emphasized special groups. The first Saturday of each month was devoted to 4-H clubs; the second, to land grant colleges; the third, to the National Grange; and the fourth, to the American Farm Bureau Federation. NBC underwrote all costs.[10]

Much of the program's format came from lessons learned from the experimental Montgomery Ward program and suggestions made at the third Advisory Council meeting on January 30, 1929. Farrell cited the Starch Reports on radio listeners, noting, "Dr. Starch's investigation shows impressively the preference of the rural audience not only for talks on crops and market reports, but also for the best music, plays, religious service, children's programs, educational service and informational talks on general subjects."[11] The type of program, then, could appeal to both rural and urban audiences.

The Advisory Council's formal report and subsequent press releases emphasized the particular attention NBC was to pay to agricultural and educational programs in the future. NBC would continue its public service through initiating specific, daily agricultural shows and expanding educational endeavors for high school, college and university, and adult audiences. Aylesworth reported, "Two of the most important services rendered through the National Broadcasting Company upon policies laid down by subcommittees of the Advisory Council pertain to religion and agriculture."[12]

Before the new *Farm and Home* program began on July 8, NBC asked Farrell for comments to include in its publicity. He telegraphed NBC, noting, "The farm audience has demonstrated a high average quality in the preference it has shown for high class programs in music and other arts as well as for programs in agriculture and home economics. The providing of the farm and home radio program undoubtedly will prove to be a valuable public service."[13] His statement and those from farm organizations complimenting the network's efforts were included in NBC's press releases announcing the *National Farm and Home* program. (NBC added the word "National" to the formal title to emphasize the broad range of the program's coverage, but later the network dropped the term.)

Twenty-five stations picked up the broadcast, and at the end of the first show, NBC's Frank Mullen thanked all who had helped form the series, especially "Francis Farrell, president of Kansas State Agricultural College, who, as the agricultural member of the National Broadcasting Company's

Advisory Council, has given invaluable advice in formulating a radio service for our farm people."[14] By fall, thirty-one stations were airing the program, and NBC had started a special agricultural network designed to reach more than seven million farmers in the Mississippi River valley. Affiliate WLS in Chicago, owned by the weekly magazine *Prairie Farmer*, was the originating station. In addition to informative and entertaining programs sponsored both by commercial clients and by NBC, this new specialized network also carried the *Farm and Home* program as part of its six A.M. to six P.M. hours of operation.[15]

In general, what NBC dubbed the "Farm Network" existed as a specialized commercial network for those companies and services wishing to reach Midwest farmers.[16] During 1929 NBC carried nearly three hundred programs having to do directly with agriculture, up from seventy-five in 1928. The network continued to pick up affiliates for its agricultural programs. By January 1930 forty-one stations comprised a coast-to-coast network airing what was now called the *Farm and Home Hour*. It and all other agriculturally oriented programs were carried at NBC's expense "as an editorial contribution and service to agriculture." The expansion followed the Advisory Council's recommendations made in 1928, and "the *Farm and Home Hour* in particular, while designed primarily to convey information to the farmer, proved to have considerable influence in promoting urban and rural relations and music appreciation." NBC planned to continue these successful broadcast arrangements in 1930. It also planned to present special, regionalized material for different sections of the country.[17]

Farrell presented these figures at the Advisory Council's fourth meeting on January 29, 1930. His formal report noted NBC's accomplishments in 1929 and its plans for 1930 mentioned in previous paragraphs.[18] The council noted all the reports and then spent most of its time discussing the complaints of the American Birth Control League over denial of time for coverage of its birth control conference the previous November. That important decision is covered in chapter 5.

By the council's fifth meeting on January 28, 1931, two members had resigned: Charles Evans Hughes upon his appointment as Chief Justice of the Supreme Court and Charles MacFarland upon his retirement from active service with the Federal Council of Churches of Christ in America. With these departures, the other council members considered replacements and additions to the council. Newton Baker and Dr. Henry Sloane Coffin were elected unanimously to the council to succeed Hughes and MacFarland, respectively.

Born in Martinsburg, West Virginia, in 1871, Newton Baker practiced law and politics in Cleveland as a protégé of Tom Loftin Johnson, four-term mayor of Cleveland and a member of Congress from 1891 to 1895. Baker served as the city's solicitor from 1902 to 1912, when he became mayor. As solicitor, he opposed the powerful public utilities, and as mayor, he instituted important tax reforms. In March 1917 President Woodrow Wilson appointed him secretary of war, even though he was an avowed pacifist. He left public office in 1921 and entered private law practice in Cleveland but remained a public figure. An ardent advocate of peace, he urged U.S. entry into the League of Nations, and in 1928 President Calvin Coolidge appointed him to the Permanent Court of Arbitration, or the Hague Tribunal.

Born in New York City in 1877, Henry Sloane Coffin was president of the Union Theological Seminary from 1926 to 1945. He began his theological career as a lecturer at the seminary in 1904 and pastor at the Madison Avenue Presbyterian Church in New York City in 1905. From 1943 to 1944 he was moderator of the General Assembly of the Presbyterian Church in the USA.

In addition to these two men, the council believed it leaned too much to the moderate-conservative side. The members formed a committee of Root, O'Brien, and Green to look into whether the council would "be more representative, and therefore stronger, if one or two members were elected who could serve as spokesmen for the more liberal and radical movements in the social field." The committee was charged with selecting the best-qualified liberal individual.[19]

NBC president Merlin Aylesworth reported that in 1930 NBC provided programs for an average of eighteen hours per day over its networks. In the typical broadcast day, hours devoted to commercial programs comprised about one-third of the airtime, with the other two-thirds carrying sustaining programs. Seventy-four stations were linked via a permanent wire network of 34,500 miles, and gross revenues for 1930 exceeded $22 million. The primary programming concerns facing members were educational broadcasts, religious programming, shows for farmers and rural areas, and broadcasts aimed at women.[20] Underpinning all programming was advertising, which during the council's meeting, Root observed, "was the supposed price which we paid for free programs."[21] In other words, if an American owned a radio set, he or she could receive the shows for no additional cost.

In response, Owen Young contrasted the American system with that of the British Broadcasting Company. The BBC was financed by both a tax levied on all radio sets and sale of a radio magazine it published. This periodical competed with others for advertising and provided readers with the most useful information on radio programs, as the British press was allowed to carry only brief announcements of programs. Consequently, the magazine had a large circulation and was a highly attractive advertising outlet. Young added that BBC officials "quite frankly upheld the principle of an intelligent dictatorship to give the public not what it wants but what, in the opinion of the officials, it ought to have." In contrast, he noted, was "the American idea of attempting to find out what the public wants and encouraging the public to determine the programs."[22]

Root expressed a profound distrust of a BBC-type system that put the government in control of radio. He felt "the danger . . . was that abuse of such a system might lead to the strangling of criticism." No matter how enlightened the dictator, little or no protection existed against the unscrupulous despot. He concluded "by and large, democratic principles were the only real protection for the people." Members also observed the fifteen million sets in use in the United States were owned by all segments of American society.[23]

Farrell's report on agricultural programming stated that broadcasts were essentially of the same nature as the year before. Of note was the expansion of the *National Farm and Home Hour* to an actual hour from the forty-five minutes allotted earlier and coverage of two international agricultural events—the World Poultry Congress in London and the first American 4-H Club girls' international chorus presentation, again from London. During the regular broadcasts an orchestra of eleven presented music of all kinds—from instrumental to patriotic to folk—to its audience. Vocal artists added to this melodic entertainment. Over the next few years, musical entertainment followed the pattern set in 1930 with a variety of orchestra, instrumental, and vocal acts. No dance music or jazz, however, was included in the program, as NBC did not consider these melodic forms "high class." Instead, musical numbers included at least one operatic selection, with the balance coming from traditional ballads, light operas, and, what NBC called "musical comedies," such as Broadway shows.[24]

Government agencies cooperated with NBC in providing informational material for this show, as well as numerous other programs aimed at rural listeners. Much of this agricultural broadcasting was offered on a sustaining basis at a cost of approximately $1 million to NBC and its affiliates. At Farrell's suggestion, NBC had expanded coverage up and down the Pacific Coast with the *Western Farm and Home Hour*. He had also suggested these programs, broadcast over the noon hour Pacific time, emphasize concerns pertinent to the region, including conservation and issues revolving around public domain lands.[25]

In 1931 the *Farm and Home Hour* inaugurated a daily weather forecast furnished for the eastern half of the country by the U.S. Weather Bureau. These forecasts for the next twenty-four to thirty-six hours supplemented the weather summaries of the previous twenty-four hours already presented on the *Hour*. Frank Mullen thought the step was "one of the most progressive movements we have made in the *National Farm and Home Hour*."[26] Other developments included programs to promote community singing among rural children and their parents, talks about commercial fertilizers, and coverage of both the Rural Scout program and the American Country Life Association. When Farrell reviewed these accomplishments, he noted the absence of "dramatic methods" for presenting information he and other members of the Advisory Council had recommended to NBC at its January 1931 meeting. At that time, he and others had noted how well sketches presented information in an entertaining fashion. He believed dramatic methods were essential in reaching audiences, especially young people.[27] Such sketches became a regular part of the *Hour* in January 1932 with "Uncle Sam's Forest Rangers," which portrayed the work of the Forest Service for younger audiences.[28]

By fall 1931 NBC had negotiated for exclusive rights to present numerous agricultural events for the next year, including the National Dairy Show, the National Corn Husking Contest, Future Farmers of America annual meeting and speech contest, the International Live Stock Exposition, and the annual conventions of the National Grange, the American Farm Bureau Federation, and the Land Grant College Association. A special twelve-week series of programs took aim at the prevention of farm fires, which cost about $150 million annually. In September the *Farm and Home Hour* and the agricultural press also helped NBC publicize the upcoming third season of Damrosch's *Music Appreciation Hour*, set to begin on Friday, October 9, from 11 A.M. to noon eastern time.[29]

But the fall of 1931 also saw changes in the *Farm and Home Hour*. Following a controversial talk from the Farmers Union on the *Hour*, the USDA demanded changes be made, as government officials, including Secretary of Agriculture Arthur Hyde, believed "the public regarded all *Farm and Home Hours* as Department (of Agriculture) utterances." Now programs presented by farm organizations on Saturdays had to be labeled by their respective names, such as *The Farmers' Union Hour*, *The American Farm Bureau Hour*, or *The National Grange Hour*, and the programs had to be dissociated from the *Farm and Home Hour*.[30]

As the Depression deepened and the 1932 presidential campaign approached, NBC initiated another weekly program, *The NBC Farm Forum*, in the time slot following the *Hour*. The *Forum* had evolved in direct response to complaints from business interests that the *Farm and Home Hour* devoted too much time to government policies and was, therefore, one-sided in reaching rural listeners, who constituted nearly half of the U.S. population. In the midst of the 1932 presidential campaign, many farm issues were political in nature and, therefore, controversial. Frank Mullen had met with USDA officials in early June 1932 to discuss the issue. The department was adamant that no other groups be allowed to offer their ideas on the *Farm and Home Hour*, which the USDA viewed as "its" program. The new *Forum* would allow discussion of controversial farm issues in a venue not associated in listeners' minds with the USDA.[31] Listeners tuned in to the program with enthusiasm, and Mullen believed *The Farm Forum* had "solved several vexatious problems" and was "rendering an absolutely impartial service first to the farmers and then to those business interests which disagree with some of the present-day agriculture policies." It also allowed NBC to maintain its impartiality in an election year.[32]

By early 1933 the *Farm and Home Hour* had grown in importance and was the most popular sustaining program NBC carried. Nonagricultural organizations, including government bodies, asked for time on the program to reach rural audiences with important information. NBC tried to accommodate such requests to the benefit of the audience. For example, the Department of Interior ran a series of reports on the findings of the Interior's Committee on the Costs of Medical Care, including medical costs in rural areas, while the Post Office presented weekly talks, stressing the value of rural free delivery and parcel post.[33]

Speeches dominated much of the 1932 programming, with the USDA presenting 572 talks and other speakers giving 442 talks. In addition, NBC also found that "the interview method of broadcasting," as well as dramatic sketches, greatly enhanced the program and provided stimulating ways to disperse material. In his formal report on the 1932 broadcast year, Mullen noted that using interviews "was one of the principal achievements of the year" and noted that NBC planned more extensive use of the interview format in 1933.[34] Mullen acknowledged and thanked Farrell for his suggestion in the 1931 Advisory Council report that both "conversational (interview) and dramatic methods" be used "so as to increase the interest and effectiveness of farm programs." NBC and the USDA had received more than a half million letters from rural families showing appreciation for the information and entertainment the *Farm and Home Hour* conveyed.[35]

At the time, with little to no research available for determining audience size, networks used a gauge of one letter to ten listeners to determine program popularity. NBC reasoned that at a minimum, five million radio families listened to the program. This figure was substantial, given that the U.S. Census listed thirty million households in the U.S. in 1930 and that 60 percent of these families, both urban and rural, had radio sets at the time.[36]

In 1933 NBC found the *Farm and Home Hour* even more important in reaching rural listeners with information on President Franklin Roosevelt's New Deal. At the seventh Advisory Council meeting February 1, 1933, Farrell advised the addition of a regular feature in the *Farm and Home Hour* "to provide an unbiased presentation of the essential facts relating to pending Federal [*sic*] legislation of special importance to agricultural and rural life."[37] He reported NBC's 1932 agricultural offerings were "conspicuously successful." While not much changed materially from the 1931 season, several important improvements were made, including an increase in government and private agencies using the *National Farm and Home Hour* to reach rural audiences during the Depression, a merger of the Monday through Friday *Western Farm and Home Hour* with the *National Farm and Home Hour* on Saturdays to bring western programs to national audiences, and inclusion of a wider variety of features in both programs to prevent monotony in the schedule. During the summer and fall, a new program based on the 1932 *Farm Forum* program and called by the same name presented controversial topics, such as purposely cutting farm production and the concept of cooperative marketing, in which farmers banded together to sell their agricultural products collectively. Special events such as the Michigan Cherry Festival and International Live Stock Exposition were also carried. Suggestions for improvement for the next year included programs on pending federal legislation that affected rural life and on noneconomic interests, such as music and home beautification.[38] Within weeks of FDR's inauguration, the *Hour* was covering increased congressional legislative activities aimed at alleviating the Depression's effects on the farm economy.[39]

With the problems facing the American farmer, the *Farm and Home Hour* drew fire from all sides for presenting Roosevelt's controversial agriculture agenda. As with the Hoover administration, FDR's administration believed the Monday-through-Friday *Hour* programs were "their" shows, their mouthpiece, and did not want anything potentially embarrassing to the USDA broadcast.[40] The Saturday programs, of course, were still produced by 4-H and farm organizations. NBC, however, regarded the program as one of its sustaining programs, offered to listeners as a public service, with only the fifteen minutes of news from Washington under the USDA's control. Mullen wanted to separate clearly the USDA segment of the program in the minds of listeners from those underwritten by NBC, but he was urged to wait until the end of the special congressional session and disposition of the farm bills then under consideration. Then changes would not "throw us into dispute with everyone wanting to take part" in the debate. In addition, any "move right now might alienate the goodwill which we have built up in the Department [of Agriculture]."[41]

Farrell was kept apprised of the situation, and at the next Advisory Council meeting more than one year later, he reported that "the *Farm Forum* has been adopted successfully as a method of dealing with the difficult question of broadcasting highly controversial discussions." A total of twenty-two programs were broadcast, and speakers represented a wide range of opinions, from those calling for a "farmers' strike" to those representing the railroads carrying farm products to markets.[42]

As for the *Farm and Home Hour*, he said the fifty-eight stations carrying the program provided listeners excellent coverage of crucial agricultural topics. In like fashion, the *Western Farm and Home Hour*, carried by ten stations along the Pacific Coast and in western states, proved informative and entertaining for listeners in that region. He contrasted the efforts seven years earlier, when NBC carried a total of only forty station hours and about fifty speakers in three agricultural broadcasts, with 1933, when NBC carried approximately seventeen thousand station hours and nearly one thousand speakers.[43]

In 1933 the USDA used the *Hour* extensively to inform listeners about implementation of the Agricultural Adjustment Administration (AAA) Act. Congress passed the act to help alleviate the Depression farm crisis by increasing prices through control of crop production. Explaining this administration farm policy on radio was, according to Farrell, "one of the most important uses made of the Company's [NBC] agricultural broadcasting service during 1933."[44]

In a letter of commendation to NBC, Milton Eisenhower, director of the USDA's information office, cited the rapid speed of cotton farmers' understanding of AAA's policy.. He said, "All the facts about [cotton] contracts, options, what could be done with retired acreage, the probable benefit payments, how payments were to be made, the system of local administration, and related items were all explained in radio talks. The fact that nearly one million farmers understood the program and participated in it, all within a period of four weeks, is evidence that they obtained accurate information."[45]

In addition to material from the USDA, the *Hour's* audience heard entertainment and information related to agriculture sponsored by the Post Office, farm newspapers and magazines, land grant colleges, the American Farm Bureau, the National Grange, the Farmers Educational and Cooperative Union, and the Future Farmers of America. Twenty-nine other organizations, including the Izaak Walton League, the American

Public Health Association, the National Home Library Foundation, and the National Education Association, contributed occasionally to the program. Musical numbers, especially folk music, and speakers with a general audience appeal expanded the audience to more than just farm families. All in all, listeners heard what Farrell deemed "one of the best and most popular radio programs in the world" that supplied "high-class musical, literary, and dramatic features" in addition to vital information to its audience.[46] Farrell recommended NBC continue its current daytime broadcast schedule and add an occasional evening program, as such nighttime programs would reach and inform city audiences about agricultural issues to a greater extent than regular midday shows.[47]

NBC readily adopted Farrell's suggestion for nighttime programs, and in 1934 NBC's Red and Blue networks carried fifteen addresses on thirteen evenings. Most originated in Washington, D.C., and presented information and discussion on the AAA and its impact on farmers and urban consumers alike. In his report for the ninth council meeting, Farrell praised NBC for its fairness in all its programming, both nighttime and daytime, presenting controversial issues related to agriculture.[48]

By the mid-1930s one of the biggest problems facing the *Farm and Home Hour* and the *Western Farm and Home Hour* was the shifting of their broadcast hours during daylight savings time. For the most part, farmers preferred to maintain the programs on standard time. When NBC tried to meet that preference, it ran into objections from affiliates on the Red Network that carried sponsored daytime programs. By 1937 NBC was trying with some success to shift both farm programs to its Blue Network, which carried most of NBC's sustaining programs. One of the biggest problems with the Blue Network affiliates was that they did not have the extensive coverage area of their Red Network counterparts, many of which were clear-channel stations.[49]

By the time the *Farm and Home Hour* celebrated its three-thousandth show on June 7, 1938, it had moved largely to the Blue Network and was carried coast-to-coast, eliminating the need for a separate *Western Hour*.[50] Now renamed *The National Farm and Home Hour*, the program continued its format of music, sketches, and speakers from government agencies and farm organizations. Its three-thousandth program illustrates the appeal of the series to both rural and urban audiences. From NBC studios in Chicago, the announcer welcomed the audience and introduced a series of musical numbers—first a male soloist, followed by Victor Herbert's *American Fantasy* medley, then the Vass Family quintet, and last of all, a female soloist. Then the announcer introduced the *Hour's* first speaker, "Dr. Francis Farrell, president of Kansas State College in Manhattan, Kansas, and a member of the Advisory Council of the National Broadcasting Company." The network switched to Manhattan, Kansas. After Farrell's five-minute address, the network switched back to Chicago for other songs and then to Washington, D.C., for an address from Secretary of Agriculture Henry Wallace, followed by another speech from NBC president Lenox Lohr in New York. Music and sketches rounded out the program.[51]

At the end of the summer, the *Hour* announced it would take a new form, beginning September 26. The last fifteen minutes would present information important to five different regions of the country. In three of the regions—Corn Belt/Northern Plains, Western Cotton Belt/Southern Plains, and New England/Middle Atlantic States—Goodyear Tire and Rubber Company would sponsor the remaining time. NBC would produce programs for the other two regions—the Southern Cotton Belt and Pacific Coast/Intermountain states—with the hope of selling the time to other advertisers in the future. Goodyear declined sponsorship in those two regions because of the poor purchasing power in the South and the early morning time the *Hour* aired live on the West Coast. The Goodyear plan departed from the original *Hour* approach, first in being sponsored and second in emphasizing the nation's regions.[52]

Changes in technology now allowed networks to carry different signals during the same broadcast time to stations around the country. The popularity of the *Hour* in the early 1930s had always attracted potential sponsors, and now changes in the broadcast industry enabled NBC officials to contemplate changing the network's approach to carrying sustaining programs in lieu of sponsored shows. In the past NBC had resisted any sponsorship of the *Hour* because of the objections of the various national associations and government agencies that participated in the hour-long program. Those nonprofit and government concerns, especially the USDA, did not want their names attached to any commercial entity, and collectively they had applauded NBC's efforts in producing the program as evidence of the network's commitment to the public service mandate required in the Communications Act of 1934.

In fact, in 1934 during FCC hearings on the need for facilities for nonprofit broadcasting, USDA administrators and other government officials had testified in favor of keeping the current broadcast setup. They saw such a set-aside as unnecessary because "the experience of the Department of Agriculture—particularly with the *National Farm and Home Hour*—gave indication that commercial broadcasters would provide facilities for cultural, educational, and informational programs." Now, several years later,

NBC felt the pressure of its affiliates' desire to sell time during the popular noon hour. Consequently, the network planned to include the government agencies and nonprofits only in the first forty-five minutes of the sustaining show distributed nationwide.[53] The audience had become too attractive to advertisers for NBC not to sell the program, if possible.

The USDA, which had participated in the *Hour* since its inception, had not been consulted about the change, and its officials were furious. In letters to NBC officials, they strenuously objected to the Goodyear sponsorship of what they saw as a segment of "their" program. They also wrote Farrell, who sent a separate letter of complaint to NBC president Lenox Lohr. Farrell recognized the great pressure Lohr was under to produce increased financial returns, especially with the lucrative farm market built through the *Hour*'s popularity. He believed the noncommercial basis of the program, instead of commercial sponsorship, was one of the reasons for the success "of one of the most useful, if not the most useful, radio programs" NBC carried.[54]

The letter arrived when Lohr was on vacation, so James Angell, NBC's educational counselor, replied "to assure [Farrell] that the Farm and Home Hour is a program in which the National Broadcasting Company has the deepest interest, as is well evidenced by the many years in which, in the face of many difficulties, it has kept the program on the air." He added that "whatever changes may ultimately be introduced, you can be sure that the unquestioned values in the program will be protected and preserved—and I believe increased."[55]

When he returned from vacation, Lohr wrote Farrell with assurances that the *Hour* would continue but that the Goodyear sponsorship would begin as planned. He implored Farrell to listen to the new-format show and when he had heard "enough of the new series to give a fair sample of the Goodyear contribution, I hope you will give me the benefit of any suggestions you may have."[56] Farrell had no negative reaction to the new format. The next summer the *Hour* returned to its full, sustaining hour-long format, but by fall, with the outbreak of war in Europe, the *Hour* became forty-five minutes again.[57]

Over the next few years, as U.S. involvement in the war became more likely, the *Farm and Home Hour* began carrying programs with a national defense emphasis. NBC also began a new series, titled *American Agriculture Mobilizes*, that concentrated on problems facing farmers as they attempted to meet specific goals and plans for increased production. In 1941 the "Food for Freedom" campaign was initiated throughout the country. By November the *Farm and Home Hour* was recorded in Hollywood for distribution on the West Coast the next morning at six. Farmers liked this new time, but urbanites were "unhappy over the change."[58] After America entered the war, NBC had "to maintain as elastic a schedule as possible to take care of any additional demands by the Department of Agriculture as a result of the national emergency."[59]

While the successful *Farm and Home Hour* eventually attracted sponsors and maintained a core audience throughout the Depression and war years, another program begun at the suggestion of council member Walter Damrosch in 1928 achieved a smaller but no less devoted audience. The *Music Appreciation Hour* became one of radio's most successful educational, in-school program series.

Music Appreciation Hour

Created and hosted by Walter Damrosch, the *Music Appreciation Hour* was designed to supplement, not supplant, existing classroom music appreciation courses by presenting music otherwise unavailable to the typical Depression-era schoolroom.[60] In its first year the *Music Hour* distributed instructors' manuals with a letter explaining the program to all school superintendents in every state, except Washington, Oregon, and California. NBC believed these states would receive the program too early in the day to be included in curricula, so it did not intentionally broadcast the live program to West Coast schools. Before the series began in September 1929, NBC broadcast promotional materials, telling teachers how they could obtain manuals and informing interested listeners how they could get a "program booklet" to follow the series. By December 31, 1929, 46,564 manuals had been sent out, while the number of program booklets totaled 13,403. NBC estimated five million students listened to the program weekly.[61]

After it began, NBC received more than ten thousand letters about the program, many with suggestions for improving the presentations, including publicizing the series as soon as possible and completing an instructor's manual by May so school boards could use the program in their curriculum. Other letters requested Damrosch's comments on the musical selections, so NBC collected his remarks and sent them to more than three hundred educational journals with permission to publish the material. In later years initial summaries of Damrosch's perspectives on the selections were included in the manuals. Program notes were also sent to NBC's publicity department, which sent them to newspapers and other periodicals, including the monthly digest of radio programs, *What's on the Air.*[62]

Observations of in-classroom use showed that the musical programs were most successful when "the children have been previously prepared and the teacher acts as mediator" in directing the children's listening. Therefore, NBC concluded teachers' manuals should state facts and background concisely so teachers could organize their own questions using their own teaching methods.[63] Future *Music Appreciation Hour* resources included such preparatory materials as background on the composers, program notes on the musical selections, and topics for possible classroom discussion. In addition, NBC prepared a separate student notebook and made it available through publisher Carl Fischer, Inc.[64]

To further publicize the program to schools, NBC representatives spoke to the New York Music Teachers Association on February 18, 1930, and attended the National Education Association conference later that month. NBC's publicity department sent out several press releases on the 1930–31 school year series that newspapers and magazines ran. The number of letters the program received from September 1 to December 31, 1930, was nearly 70 percent higher than those received during the same period in 1929. That fall, just under forty-eight thousand teacher's manuals and nearly thirty-one thousand program booklets were distributed to teachers and listeners, respectively.[65] Over the years the teacher notebooks grew in sophistication so that by the end of the decade the teacher's guides included instructions for understanding and presenting each selection to the appropriate grades. At the back of each guide was a bibliographic list of textbooks, music manuals, analytic materials, and records related to topics covered.[66]

Student notebooks cost one dime and were divided into four class levels—series A for beginners, series B for more advanced elementary students, and series C and D for high school students. Broadcasts of each series lasted one-half hour, and series A and B alternated weeks with series C and D. So the fall season began with the series A program, followed by the series B lesson. The next week began with a series C session, followed by series D. Over the years, student notebooks grew in size from five-by-eight-inch to eight-by-ten-inch pamphlets, and small pocket-sized booklets were offered to the general public. From the demand of these small guides in the 1932–33 school year, NBC estimated one-third of its audience for the *Music Appreciation Hour* was the general public. Indeed, many music clubs focused on Damrosch's concerts, and the official magazine of the National Federation of Music Clubs contained complimentary reviews of the *Hour*.[67] Interest was so great that by 1935 NBC had even given permission to the American Red Cross to publish the student notebooks in Braille,[68] and the company also worked with publishing houses and record companies to supply school orchestras and chorus groups with sheet music and phonograph recordings to complement the broadcasts.[69]

All of these developments resulted from advancements in broadcast technology and sound recording. At the council's fifth meeting in January 1931, Walter Damrosch's official report emphasized the technical improvements made in broadcasting music,[70] and he suggested NBC aid the development of jazz, "a real American art form," through offering a prize "to stimulate composers to do for jazz what Schubert, Brahms, and Strauss did for the waltz." According to the minutes, Young and the council "warmly approved" the suggestion and commended it to Aylesworth for appropriate action,[71] but no prize was ever offered.

The council cited the *Music Appreciation Hour* as a significant contribution to the betterment of American education. University of Virginia president Edwin Alderman believed NBC had done well in presenting such programs of educational significance in music and drama. He also considered that groups like the National Advisory Council on Radio in Education (NACRE), under the direction of Levering Tyson, justified NBC's policy of waiting for educators to organize for presentation of comprehensive educational programs. To that end, Tyson had been invited to the meeting and presented the council an outline of the work, plans, and purposes of NACRE. He then led an informal discussion of the possibilities for education through radio. Tyson noted NACRE, established on May 12, 1930, "was interested primarily in the formation and presentation of really authoritative educational programs." At that time he was organizing committees to deal with issues in general educational subject areas, such as music, drama, literature, and science. He added that when it came to broadcast facility use, his group would be interested in obtaining the best available facilities, whether they were commercial or academic.[72]

At the next year's meeting, in February 1932, Merlin Aylesworth noted that twelve additional stations had become NBC affiliates, including KGH in Honolulu, connected to the West Coast via RCA's shortwave radio facilities. These additional stations increased the number of wired miles to 38,500, and NBC's gross revenues reached $29.5 million. Aylesworth believed the greatest radio development in 1931, however, was refining and broadening the scope of programming. A review of programming for January 1932 revealed musical shows comprised 62 percent of the schedule; educational programs, including information and public service, constituted 21 percent; literature and drama, 15 percent; and religion, 2 percent. Of special note, he said, was the *Music Appreciation Hour*, which aired live at eleven A.M. eastern time and eight A.M. Pacific time on Friday. During the fall of 1931, schools and colleges requested sixty-five thousand instructors' manuals, and NBC realized that for each instructor's manual more than one hundred students were taking the course. In addition, another new program, *Radio Guild,* presented plays selected from school and college reading lists, and schools all over the country used them in conjunction with classroom study.[73]

The Advisory Council's 1932 report from its committee on education proved of most importance because of an ongoing Federal Radio Commission's inquiry into commercialism and education in radio. This investigation came as the result of the Couzen-Dill Resolution passed by the U.S. Senate in 1931. In the field of "pure education" NBC executives believed "the initiative and responsibility for the program should rest in the hands of the educators, with the Company furnishing its facilities free of charge. Radio broadcasting, however, can and does offer, and perhaps is best fitted for, educational programs which supplement and complement the work of the classroom." Working with Levering Tyson and NACRE, NBC carried a series of weekly programs on two subjects, psychology and economics. Prominent individuals in each field devised the programs, and the productions were patterned somewhat after the successful *Music Appreciation Hour.*[74]

Through cooperation of the University of Chicago Press and the American Library Association, listeners of the shows could obtain reading lists, reprints of addresses, and "Listener's Notebooks" free of charge or at a nominal price. In the first ten weeks of the series, nearly one hundred thousand requests for reading material had been received. Listener groups also formed out of both mutual interest in the topics and classes offered as a supplement to established university programs. NBC viewed these programs as demonstrating the acceptability of such courses of study when presented in a comprehensive, purposeful design specifically made for radio. Of course, supplementing these more traditional programs were those that both entertained and enlightened, such as the *Music Appreciation Hour* and the *Radio Guild,* or those that presented current events and issues of public interest.[75]

In other business, the council chose new members to replace the three who had died during the previous year: Edwin Alderman, Dwight Morrow, and Julius Rosenwald. Dr. Robert Maynard Hutchins of the University of Chicago and Mr. Felix Warburg of New York were elected to fill the vacancies. The choice of a third member was deferred to a committee headed by Elihu Root. As mentioned earlier, that committee had been charged with selecting "the best-qualified liberal" for council membership to expand the viewpoints represented on the council.[76] Walter Lippman was suggested, but he declined because, as a journalist, he saw a potential conflict of interest, as he might have to comment on the radio industry or on NBC's specific policies.[77]

Both Hutchins and Warburg joined the council immediately after the 1932 meeting. Hutchins replaced Alderman and was by far the youngest member on the council. Robert Hutchins became president of the University of Chicago at age thirty in 1929. In 1945, he became chancellor, a position he held until 1951. Born in Brooklyn, New York, on January 17, 1899, Hutchins studied at Oberlin College and graduated from Yale in 1921. He taught law at Yale from 1925 to 1927, becoming dean in 1927. After 1943 he served as chairman of the board of editors for the *Encyclopedia Britannica*. Always interested in adult education, Hutchins took a year's leave of absence in 1946 to promote the "great books" program initiated by Chicago attorney and industrialist Lynn A. Williams. The next year he became chairman of the Commission on Freedom of the Press. He was associate director of the Ford Foundation from 1951 to 1954, when he became president of the Fund for the Republic. Hutchins later founded the Center for the Study of Democratic Institutions in Santa Barbara, California, and from 1969 to 1974 was its chairman. His books include *The Higher Learning in America* and *Education for Freedom*, published in 1936 and 1943, respectively. He died May 15, 1977.

Felix Warburg was a well-known banker and philanthropist and was selected to replace Rosenberg as the Jewish voice on the council. In 1894 Warburg emigrated from Hamburg, Germany, where he was born into a renowned Jewish financial family on January 14, 1871. With his older brother Paul, Warburg joined the firm of Kuhn, Loeb & Company, and in 1895 he married Frieda Schiff, daughter of philanthropist Jacob Schiff. They had five children. In the 1930s Warburg was known for patronage of education, music, and the arts, as well as his humanitarian work after World War I and his aid in expatriating Jews after the Nazis came to power in Germany. In the fifteen years before his death on October 20, 1937, he and his wife gave away more than $13 million to charity, education, and civic organizations. As with Rosenberg, Warburg supported several black organizations, including the NAACP and the Tuskegee Institute.

Both Warburg and Hutchins came to the next council meeting on February 1, 1933. Hutchins had been named chair of the council's educational committee. In his report he noted the proposals then in Congress for setting aside 15 percent of the spectrum for educational stations. He believed that NBC "must work toward a policy of treating educational programs in the same way as commercial programs as to hours, days, and the definiteness of all (program production) arrangements. . . . [I] t is my opinion that during this period of technical and experimental development educators can do no better than to utilize, wherever possible, existing facilities." At the same time, he asked that the council and NBC continue to study what was being done in other countries regarding educational programming and to adapt constructive policies to the American situation.[78]

In 1932 network executives and educators planned educational programs far more in advance than they had previously. In 1932 NBC guaranteed NACRE and the National Education Association time for their educational series through June 1934. Positive response to NBC's *Music Appreciation Hour* assured its continuation, and enthusiastic feedback to the twenty-five operas broadcast from the New York City Metropolitan Opera ensured coverage in 1933 and 1934. In fact, Aylesworth counted bringing the world's greatest operas into American homes as one of NBC's outstanding achievements.[79]

Aylesworth also noted that 1932 saw a greater variety of entertainment programs offered to audiences. With the growth of these shows and "under existing economic conditions [the fact] prices had a definite interest for the listening public," NBC altered its policy on commercials giving the cost of goods and services. He told the council members that this change resulted from "a conviction on our part that direct mention of prices would be more acceptable to the radio audience than the long and monotonous statements which often resulted from the effort to avoid mentioning them [prices]." He saw the public's ready acceptance of this policy as justifying NBC's decision.[80]

Educators struggled with presentation of programs, finding the straight lecture too boring and attempts at scripted spontaneity for roundtable and question-and-answer formats too obvious. Printed guides and suggested reading lists to help overcome these shortcomings were suggested. Programs such as the *Music Appreciation Hour* with its accompanying texts and notebooks supplemented regular school classes, and the council's educational subcommittee lauded its success. *The Radio Guild*'s repertory adapted plays for hour-long presentations each week, and the Advisory Council recommended supplying supplementary textual material similar to that supplied for the *Music Hour*, if the demand warranted. Symphonic concerts, especially those under the direction of council member Walter Damrosch, and broadcasts on scientific topics, the world of art, and the fields of literature, history, and public affairs enlightened the public.[81]

With more than 60 percent of airtime devoted to music, Walter Damrosch's report noted that programming reflected fewer innovations during 1932 than in previous years. But, he added, music programs made "steady progress along lines already laid out and a tendency to reaffirm and develop policies previously established." In last year's report Damrosch urged increase in carriage of chamber music and symphonic orchestras. He was pleased to report more numerous programs in both forms, as well as expansion of opera performances, which had been limited for technical reasons to presentation of one or two acts, to full performances. He especially congratulated NBC on its music education programs, as economic conditions forced many schools to drop music education. "Radio can and must help to keep alive the interest in music so carefully fostered [during the past twenty-five years] by thousands of supervisors and teachers, many of whom are now, unfortunately, unemployed," he observed.[82]

At the next year's meeting Hutchins reported on experiments with radio education commencing at the University of Chicago, where he was president. He emphasized the need for radio, especially shortwave, for educational programming. He added foundations, among others, should begin to underwrite these programs. In adult education, he noted the trend toward presentation of cultural, not vocational, courses. He congratulated the networks on their support of educational programming and expressed the hope that local stations would begin to follow network standards. Farrell compared the current agriculturally oriented programs to those offered seven years earlier, when the council first met. He marveled at both their quality and quantity, a record he found "altogether extraordinary." Similarly, Damrosch was "delighted that music had seized this opportunity [radio] to deepen its appeal." He was "particularly satisfied" that his own musical broadcasts reached more than six million school children, but he worried that lack of facilities kept another six million from hearing the concerts.[83]

Both the *Music Appreciation Hour* and the *Farm and Home Hour* reached millions of listeners. The council's members influenced, in addition to these programs, NBC's coverage of religious issues. Principal among NBC's desires was representing "the three major religions" equitably. This concern not only brought about religious program development but also advanced specific policies regarding presentation of religious shows and ideas. Both program development and the evolution of specific policies came through the work of the council's members, especially those members representing Protestantism, Catholicism, and Judaism on the council.

Religious Issues and the Advisory Council

BETWEEN THE FIRST AND SECOND Advisory Council meetings, the council's Church Committee, later renamed the Committee on Religious Activities, met several times to hammer out a draft policy for airing religious programs on NBC. The concerns expressed by O'Brien, Rosenwald, and MacFarland and the policies they developed reflected a decade of coming to grips with vast changes in family, religion, and public welfare. A clash of new and old lifestyles provoked tensions in a rapidly changing American society. Holders of traditional standards—found largely in rural areas and older, established urban centers—opposed the differing views and values of newer urban dwellers, the changing middle class, and the "flaming youth" in the younger generation.

Changes during the 1920s caused society's older authority systems to disintegrate. Social mores were rapidly altered, stimulated by Prohibition, the automobile, electrification, motion pictures, and the war experience. New and different ideas came with radio and movies, mass education, and increased mobility with the automobile. The emerging philosophy of "moral relativism" stated values were not absolute and were of human, not divine, origin. This viewpoint became the justification for scrapping older moral systems.[1]

Many churches reacted negatively to this philosophy and other drastic changes during the 1920s. In addition, new religious doctrines attempted to reconcile traditional beliefs with newer scientific evidence of the origins of the earth and of human beings. The literal interpretation of the Bible came under attack and was often abandoned in favor of seeing evolution as an act of God. Churches became more receptive to the needs of an urban, industrial society, and in doing so, they emerged as social service agencies in addition to being religious institutions. A social gospel emerged, and secular humanism vied with traditional Christian theology for societal supremacy.[2]

As religious institutions changed, World War I, urbanization, motion pictures, and the automobile brought changes in sexual customs. The war had brought Americans into contact with Old World societies that did not adhere to the more puritanical mores of America. Urbanization often gave city dwellers a more impersonal, cosmopolitan worldview and altered the authority of small-town ties and close-knit city neighborhoods. Motion pictures and fan magazines depicted different lifestyles, while the automobile brought escape from parental supervision and increased travel opportunities. All in all, the traditional Victorian codes came under intense fire during the "Jazz Age."[3]

Traditionalists attempted to defend the old societal hierarchy of WASP—white, Anglo-Saxon Protestant—superiority. To them, the United States had to be run by and for "real" Americans, defined as those WASPs believing in the older moral codes and business superiority. All other religious and ethnic groups were subordinate to WASPs, who considered Jews and Catholics engaging in conspiracies to rule America. Jews supposedly belonged to an international banking conspiracy, while Catholics were part of a papal plot to dominate America.[4] Attacks on religious views emerged because of these intense social changes. Radio emerged in this tempest, and broadcasters' program policies reflected the culture's conflicts and tensions.

Establishing Broadcast Rules for Religious Programs

A Federal Radio Commission (FRC) survey of radio programming in 1928 showed that the average station was on the air fifty-four hours per week. Of those hours, eight were devoted to religious programming,[5] and NBC and its council wanted to avoid use of the network-originated religious programs for open attacks on religion and adherents to differing religious viewpoints. From April 1927 through March 1928, the council's Committee on Religious Activities (O'Brien, Rosenwald, and MacFarland) met and corresponded with NBC executives to forge policies to avoid religious strife on radio. In consultation with Owen Young and NBC president Merlin Aylesworth, the committee developed five guiding principles. NBC readily adopted them and used them throughout the 1930s and early 1940s to combat what the network executives deemed inappropriate, tasteless, tactless, or inflammatory religious programming. Presented to the balance of the Advisory Council for its endorsement, the principles were the following:

1. NBC would "serve only the central or national agencies of the three religious faiths . . . as distinguished from individual churches or small groups where national membership was comparatively small."
2. Religious broadcasts "should be non-sectarian and non-denominational in appeal."
3. Messages should have the widest appeal, presenting the "broad claims of religion . . . which not only aid in building up the personal and social life of the individual but also aid in popularizing religion and the church."
4. Messages "should interpret religion at its highest and best" so a listener would "realize his responsibility to the organized church and to society."
5. Broadcasts should be done "by the recognized outstanding leaders of the several faiths . . ."

The committee also suggested one of NBC's programs, *University of the Air*, carry weekly evening speeches titled "Great Messages of Religion," with well-known laymen or ministers speaking. They also encouraged NBC to use speakers from cities other than New York City for regional and geographic diversity.[6]

The other Advisory Council members heartily endorsed these principles during its second meeting in March 1928. At the same meeting, council members also encouraged NBC to include religious hymns in its "educational programs," and Aylesworth suggested this might be done as part of a "children's hour" program on Sunday morning.[7]

At the following year's meeting of the Advisory Council in January 1929, Aylesworth reported NBC's religious programming had expanded, largely because of the policy the council had adopted. He noted, "Two of the most important services rendered through the National Broadcasting Company upon policies laid down by subcommittees of the Advisory Council pertain to religion and agriculture."[8] The subcommittee on religious programming reported NBC's Sunday afternoon services were well received and reiterated its endorsement of the five principles proposed and adopted the previous year for religious programming. The full council reaffirmed these principles and emphasized acceptance of shows solely from central or national agencies of Judaism, Roman Catholicism, and mainstream Protestantism. "Strictly religious" messages with wide audience appeal also had to be as nonsectarian and nondenominational as possible.[9]

This reaffirmation came, in part, as reaction to the complaint of Judge J. F. Rutherford of the People's Pulpit Association about NBC's rejection of his request to use network facilities in late summer 1928 to broadcast a ninety-minute program sponsored by the International Bible Students Association. Rutherford had appealed to the council for review of NBC's decision. While the council's review was not mentioned in its formal report, the council's handling of this issue is instructive in understanding the evolution of broadcast programming. It forcefully illustrates the pressure to present only mainstream religious principles and beliefs on the network.[10]

Judge J. F. Rutherford and the Watch Tower Society

Aylesworth gave council members background to Rutherford's protest, explaining that NBC had granted time to Judge Rutherford for a speech on July 24, 1927, "in accordance with the policy of avoiding unjust discrimination." In his speech, according to Aylesworth, Rutherford engaged in "a violent attack upon organized Christianity and its churches, and in heaping abuse upon the clergy." NBC was deluged with letters from shocked listeners from all parts of the country, Aylesworth noted, and added, for that reason, NBC's officers "had replied to subsequent applications by Judge Rutherford that they had no time available."[11]

Aylesworth also noted the question of Rutherford's access to NBC had come up several days earlier, during his testimony before the Senate Committee of Merchant Marine and Fisheries. Copies of the speech had been distributed, and Aylesworth noted the offensive nature of the speech and declared he would not permit such material to be broadcast, a statement greeted by the congressional committee with applause. Aylesworth added that NBC had never told Judge Rutherford that he was banned from the airwaves and told the senators of the Advisory Council's involvement, noting "at this time we have decided we are not looking for another of Judge Rutherford's lectures. When you ask me if we would ever furnish another one, I will have to say this Advisory Council has the power to inform me that they will approve, and I will leave it to them."[12]

Aylesworth's congressional testimony, however, had toned down and even contradicted his actual reply to Rutherford and the People's Pulpit Association. In a letter to the association, he had written,

> At the request of Judge J. F. Rutherford, your leader, the National Broadcasting Company extended its facilities for a speech by him which was delivered last July. Complete freedom was accorded to Judge Rutherford, as it is to all speakers, when facilities are extended. Judge Rutherford's speech was a rabid attack upon organized religion and the clergy of all denominations. In view of that experience, the National Broadcasting

Company cannot again permit its facilities to be used by him or his organization.[13]

Aylesworth asked for the council's views.

After some discussion, Charles Hughes suggested that "certain levels of decency must be maintained" and, without mentioning any issues regarding First Amendment principles of religious freedom or free expression, he noted NBC was "simply discharging their obligation to the public in insisting upon the observance of that standard." William Green asked whether Rutherford's organization could build a radio network of independent stations, and Aylesworth told him they probably could. Morgan O'Brien then mentioned certain denominational attacks he had heard over radio, and Aylesworth assured him these had not emanated from NBC or its owned and operated stations but rather from an independent station. Later, because Ayleswoth thought this discussion among Hughes, Green, O'Brien, and himself might be embarrassing to the council members if the report went astray, he did not include it in the council's official report.[14] What they discussed briefly, however, is instructive in showing that Aylesworth had misgivings about public reception of council members' views on keeping such a controversial, fiery speaker as Rutherford off the air.

After further discussion the council agreed that it saw no reason to interfere with NBC's verdict denying time to Rutherford and instructed Everett Case, acting secretary for the council, to inform the People's Pulpit Association that they had determined NBC had acted appropriately. Case did so the next day.[15] The People's Pulpit Association, later renamed the Watch Tower Bible and Tract Society, continued to request both free time and purchased time, which NBC always declined. In late 1931 another request to buy time led to an additional complaint to the Advisory Council, which the council reviewed during its sixth meeting.[16]

In this complaint, the society protested its inability to obtain either free or purchased time for its religious broadcasts, saying that these important proclamations contained information listeners needed and wanted. It claimed NBC stifled the organization's messages because NBC's owned and operated station WGY in Schenectady, New York, kept the society off the air. In its letter the organization warned Young of God's retribution: "In all friendliness, not threateningly, but as a warning, we invite you to consider the untimely end of your colleague H. P. Davis, who was personally responsible for terminating, without explanation, the service which Westinghouse stations KDKA and WBZ-WBZA had contracted to furnish for us."[17] In a follow-up letter, the society stated that not only had NBC refused use of its facilities but also "wrongfully prevented other radio companies from broad-casting for us." It warned "to hinder freedom of speech concerning the Bible, as is now being attempted by the National Broadcasting Company under the pretext of serving a commercial objective or 'to prevent controversy,' will work great injury to the people and justly merit the expressed indignation of Jehovah God."[18] Their intimidation did not work, and Young brought their complaint to the council's February 1932 meeting.[19]

In preparing to discuss the issue, Young's assistant, Everett Case, re-viewed the council's previous actions on prior Watch Tower complaints and noted the action the council had taken on NBC's refusal in 1930 to carry addresses of the American Birth Control League, discussed in detail in chapter 5. The principles enunciated in that situation, Case noted in a memo to Young, "would seem wholly pertinent to the subject under con-sideration. These principles implicity [sic] protect the Company against being used as a mere organ of propaganda."[20] Case gathered the relevant documents, including current letters of complaint and previous correspon-dence between NBC and the Watch Tower Society. At the meeting he read these to the council members.

In discussion John Davis argued radio could not become "the organ of a propaganda which was offensive to an overwhelming majority of its audience without destroying the medium." He noted radio was "not a common carrier in the sense that anyone can irresponsibly say anything." Green concurred and emphasized the distinctions made by Hughes and Root in the council's pronouncement on birth control coverage discussing controversial issues.[21] The council reviewed and reaffirmed the 1929 general principles guiding NBC's policies on religious programming and saw no reason to interfere with their application.[22]

After the meeting, Everett Case wrote the Watch Tower Society, stating NBC believed it could render its best service to the public by leaving determi-nation of religious programs to responsible organizations of the three major faiths—Protestant, Catholic, and Jewish. NBC's involvement lay "merely in granting the use of its facilities for such programs." Consequently, he noted, the council saw no reason to change this policy and concluded that preventing other stations from carrying Judge Rutherford had no factual basis. Case wrote that NBC owned or operated a maximum of twelve sta-tions and added that its decisions affected only those stations. NBC "has not the power, even if it had the desire, to prevent other stations from accepting any programs which their schedule and policy permit."[23]

At the end of its discussion on the Watch Tower's request, the council had also noted the accolades NBC received for its religious programs. Because many stations carried local, sustaining (and sometimes sponsored) religious programs, the Protestant, Catholic, and Jewish organizations taking advantage of NBC's offer of free airtime for their religious messages had unanimously agreed to cut time for the rotating sustaining network time to a half hour from one hour. In fact, in 1931 Jewish groups had not used their allocation, and several Protestant and Catholic groups had contracted with NBC for additional sponsored program time to bring their messages to audiences.[24] But NBC's policy to sell time to these mainstream religious groups quickly changed during 1932, as a Catholic priest, Father Charles Coughlin, sought time over the NBC and CBS networks to bring his strident messages to the public.

Father Charles Coughlin

Father Charles Coughlin originally began his broadcasts in 1926 to break down intolerance aimed at Catholics, but he soon began a popular question-and-answer session on his programs and launched into commentaries on public issues. His attacks on socialism, communism, and industrial problems and his endorsement of workers' welfare met with warm listener response, but they prompted alarmed official reaction during these Depression years. At first, three stations—one each in Detroit, Chicago, and Cincinnati—carried Father Coughlin's weekly sermons. Then, in October 1930, the broadcasts went nationwide over CBS. By year's end mail for his *Golden Hour of the Little Flower* averaged more than fifty thousand letters per week, with responses to his sermon on the Sunday before Christmas peaking at more than seventy-five thousand letters. Coughlin employed fifty-two clerical assistants to handle the correspondence, and a printing plant in Detroit published and mailed fifty thousand copies of his weekly sermons to those requesting them. Father Coughlin did not mention money over the air, leaving fund-raising for his endeavors to his Radio League of the Little Flower.[25]

Using the method then employed by broadcasters to calculate listenership—one letter writer to two hundred listeners—listeners were estimated to be more than ten million. More than half the writers were Protestant or Jewish. Even though Coughlin was later accused of anti-Semitism, in 1930, he received little adverse criticism, about two letters in one thousand, and most criticism came from Catholics. Some complaints were filed with the FRC or Coughlin's bishop, the Right Reverend Michael Gallagher of Detroit. Father Coughlin paid little heed to these critics, as he had Gallagher's approval and a letter from the Pope thanking him for his efforts in using radio.[26]

One Coughlin sermon, "Prosperity," was initially banned from broadcast over CBS on January 4, 1931. The speech attacked unemployment and economic issues, especially President Herbert Hoover's fiscal policies, and CBS asked him "to moderate his expressions as to avoid objections." Coughlin announced that CBS forbade the broadcast as an inflammatory attack on government officials, big business, and international banking. CBS denied the charges, stating they had not barred Coughlin from talking, yet admitted they had asked him to moderate his criticisms. After a week of newspaper coverage and receipt of an estimated two hundred thousand letters of protest from listeners, CBS allowed Coughlin to preach his sermon "Prosperity" over the network.[27]

Among those denouncing CBS was noted socialist Norman Thomas, who had been denied time when the priest attacked socialism over WJR. In that instance the FRC had upheld WJR's actions and replied that WJR had shown its devotion to the public interest in "preventing speakers from indulging in personalities over that station." Now Thomas "protested this gagging of his opponent,"[28] and the incident exacerbated charges of broadcaster censorship.

Later that fall, CBS did not renew Coughlin's contract, and censorship charges reemerged. After this cancellation, an editorial in the *Christian Century* decried sanctions, to which a CBS spokeswoman replied, "In connection with the recent editorial . . . inferring that freedom of speech over the radio is being denied American clergymen and citing Father Coughlin as an example of so-called censorship, we take the liberty of quoting from a telegram we have received from Father Coughlin: 'You have full liberty to state that the Columbia broadcasting system [*sic*] has at no time attempted to censure my discourse nor in any way did the Columbia broadcasting system [*sic*] try to have me removed from the air. You are free to convey this message to *The Christian Century* magazine."[29]

However, Coughlin did denounce CBS's actions over the airwaves and then set up his own independent network through WJR in Detroit. Meanwhile, CBS issued a new policy regarding religious broadcasting that echoed NBC's policies: "Columbia believes that religious broadcasting should be a public service, without remuneration . . . and has turned to the authorities of the various denominations and others apparently most competent to nominate the preachers to fill the ever-changing pulpit of the Church of the Air." CBS had asked various Catholic dioceses to select speakers, when it became their turn to appear on its *Church of the Air* program. Thus CBS had rid itself of the vexatious Coughlin.[30] The ACLU board directed Forrest

Bailey to write the FRC in connection with censorship of Father Coughlin's broadcasts,[31] yet nothing official came of these protests, as the commission stated it had no jurisdiction over this situation.

During 1932 the commission received approximately three dozen complaints about Father Coughlin's speeches and his attacks on President Hoover, but an FRC investigator found no justification for any commission action on license renewal hearings for stations carrying Coughlin's speeches. "Most of the Rev. Coughlin's remarks do not name any particular person or group and are aimed more at our national or financial system, and the principal subject discussed in all of them is revaluation of the gold standard," the investigator concluded.[32]

In April 1932 Cardinal William Henry O'Connell of Boston in a thinly veiled denunciation of Coughlin condemned "hysterical addresses from ecclesiastics" and added that it was wrong for individual priests "to address the whole world."[33] Father Coughlin asserted that he would continue his weekly broadcasts despite the cardinal's criticism, because his bishop approved them. Coughlin said that he showed the bishop his speeches the day before broadcast and added that his talks on economic and social problems were based on the writings of Popes Leo XIII and Pius XI. The New York *Times* reported that during the previous twenty-seven-week broadcast season, Coughlin received more than 2.5 million letters and added that although his parish comprised only forty-two families, ten thousand persons attend his church every Sunday.[34]

During the decade, Coughlin's attacks became far more pronounced and embarrassing to stations and church leaders. In March 1933 an alleged attack by Coughlin prompted WJR to offer free time for reply to Malcolm Bingay, editorial director of the Detroit *Free Press*. The letter stated that "the policy of this station since its organization [is] to afford equal opportunity to both sides of questions of public interest in the use of its facilities."[35] In early December 1933 complaints of possible malicious technical interference with Coughlin's programs reached the FRC. Stations and FRC field offices monitored stations carrying Coughlin's broadcasts and found no evidence of unusual interference.[36] One year later, just before Christmas, Coughlin attacked the Roosevelt administration and condemned American involvement in Mexico that began under President Woodrow Wilson's administration. From Wilson to Roosevelt, he claimed, Americans and their government tolerated and aided butchery and atheism in Mexico.[37]

Coughlin's attacks on Jews became more blatant by late 1938, when he declared Jewish internationalists and Jewish bankers responsible for both the Great War (as World War I was then known) and the Bolshevik Revolution in Russia. When the major networks declined time and other stations began to take him off the air, his listeners mounted a letter campaign to the Federal Communications Commission (FCC), the successor to the FRC. These letters protested Coughlin's inability to get airtime and asserted Coughlin's constitutional free speech rights were violated through network and station denial of time. The FCC wrote back, saying it had no power to compel stations to transmit speeches and that, by law, it could not censor licensee's programs.[38] In the meantime Coughlin set up his own network of independent stations to carry his sermons.

The NBC Advisory Council members were well aware of the CBS-Coughlin dispute by the time it held its seventh meeting in February 1933. In his report for NBC executives and the other council members, Morgan O'Brien, now chairman of the committee on religious activities, recognized overall religious organizations' contributions to overcoming low public morale during the deepening Depression and downplayed individual ministerial involvement:

> The report on Religious Broadcasting would be lacking the established facts if it failed to record and emphasize the importance of the programs under church direction during the year 1932 and their effectiveness in helping to maintain not only the nation's morale but peace and righteousness throughout the land in this unprecedented period of the country's distress. Your Committee, through its several program departments, has clearly established the fact that the people in the homes of America are now confronting greater and more difficult problems than ever before. . . .
>
> While our records show that from the beginning of radio broadcasting religious programs were received with appreciation by large numbers of the audience throughout America, the mail during the last year has increasingly indicated that men and women of every faith and creed in all walks of life are listening to the messages of religion, and that in these troublous times they are receiving a personal assistance to a higher faith and courage.[39]

These programs reflected Judeo-Christian beliefs and came from sponsoring organizations such as the Federal Council of Churches of Christ in America and the National Council of Catholic Men, not individual speakers. No Jewish group sponsored programs, however, and NBC sought to change that during 1933.[40]

By 1935 NBC was receiving letters complimenting it on its religious coverage, including the development of *Message of Israel*, a new Jewish program on Saturday night that replaced the old *Jewish Hour*.[41] The Council's subcommittee on religious broadcasting noted in both 1934 and 1935 how well NBC's religious broadcasts promoted tolerance. The principles adopted at earlier council meetings, the 1934 report read, "were not only fair but extraordinarily wise" in keeping "propagandist programs" off the air.[42] Of course, "propagandist programs" referred in large part to Father Coughlin's broadcasts.

In 1936 Father Coughlin, who had at first supported Roosevelt's New Deal policies, began an anti-FDR third-party push under his "National Union of Social Justice" banner. He believed Roosevelt had not gone far enough in his economic and monetary reforms, so he advocated economic reforms that radically challenged capitalism and contemporary political institutions. He wanted the Federal Reserve replaced with a central bank and stated the purpose of this bank was "to maintain the cost of living on an even keel and the repayment of dollar debts with equal value dollars." He promised to leave the air if his Social Justice Party received fewer than nine million votes. While he did not get even one million votes, he stayed on the air until the early 1940s to rail against the New Deal and Franklin "Double-Crossing" Roosevelt. While his core message was one of economic populism, his sermons also attacked and criticized prominent Jewish figures and seemed to defend many Nazi policies. His broadcasts were seen as evidence of anti-Semitism and became increasingly controversial for this reason. In 1942 his superiors in the Catholic Church finally forced him to stop his broadcasts and return to his work as a parish priest.[43]

When they met in 1939, Advisory Council members knew Coughlin's broadcasts had continued to be controversial. But before the meeting, Owen Young began looking for a replacement for Morgan O'Brien, who had passed away June 16, 1937, to represent the Catholic faith on the council. Young wrote the other council members to suggest that Al Smith, former New York governor and 1928 Democratic nominee for president, take O'Brien's seat. Young saw Smith as "the outstanding Catholic layman in the United States" and believed him to be the best replacement for O'Brien.[44] With the council members' unanimous consent, Young wrote Smith, inviting him to join the council. In his letter to Smith, Young included background to the council's formation, as well as a copy of the letter originally sent to all potential members in which Young outlined the problems and concerns NBC faced in networking and presenting the best possible programming to the public. "After twelve years experience, I have little to add to that letter," Young noted.[45] Smith readily accepted the invitation[46] and came to what would be the next-to-last formal council meeting on January 9, 1939.

Smith brought varied experiences to add to the council's makeup. In addition to being the unsuccessful Democratic candidate for president in 1928,

Smith had been elected to two-year terms as governor of New York in 1918, 1920, 1924, and 1926. Born into an impoverished family in New York City in 1873, Smith left school at age twelve to help support them, first working as a newsboy and then in the Fulton Fish Market. In 1895 he was appointed a clerk in the office of the county commissioner of jurors through connections in Tammany Hall. In 1904 he was elected to the New York state assembly and became speaker in 1913. As a progressive, popular governor, Smith achieved passage of much reform legislation. With the help of Franklin Roosevelt, he won the 1928 Democratic nomination for president, the first Roman Catholic to achieve this distinction. After his defeat by Herbert Hoover, Smith became president of the firm that owned and operated the Empire State Building. From 1932 to 1934 he served as editor of *New Outlook*. In the mid-1930s he became a bitter opponent of FDR's New Deal policies and supported the Republicans in 1936 and 1940.

In addition to Smith's joining the council, RCA president David Sarnoff and NBC president Lenox Lohr had asked noted educator and psychologist James Angell to oversee NBC's work with the council.[47] Born in Burlington, Vermont, in 1869, Angell graduated from the University of Michigan in 1890 and received two master's degrees, one from the University of Michigan in 1891 and the other from Harvard the following year. After study abroad, he taught at the University of Minnesota and then the University of Chicago, where he became the head of the psychology department in 1905, dean of university faculties in 1919, and acting president from 1918 to 1919. He became president of Yale in 1921, serving until his retirement in 1937. He then joined NBC as its educational counselor and a member of the NBC Advisory Council.

The council's first order of business during its January 1939 meeting was affirming the unanimous election of Smith as a council member. Later, with Father Coughlin's broadcasts in mind, Lohr presented a statement of NBC company policies that the council had previously written and approved on religious programs and coverage of controversial issues. He asked the council for its reaffirmation of these principles. He prefaced his statement with a short overview of NBC's public service policy. This summary emphasized NBC's attempts "to put on the air fine programs in every major field of interest" and noted that some subjects "present difficulties which require constant study and supervision." Such analysis and review had once again brought these policies to the council's attention. Lohr noted, "This is a world of rapidly changing philosophies, and radio is a developing art, so it is believed that these policies should be again scrutinized in the light of present-day conditions and either re-affirmed or amended."[48] He then summarized NBC's policies for religious programs, asking the council to reaffirm them.

First, he emphasized NBC did "not sell time for religious programs, as this course might result in according a disproportionate representation to those individuals or groups who chance to command the largest purses." Consequently, NBC could not serve all who wanted on the air and chose to work through "chosen responsible organizations representing the three dominant religious groups in America, i.e., Protestants, Catholics, and Jews, to suggest speakers and prepare programs." Because of this principle, NBC did not permit attacks upon religious faiths or upon racial groups, stating, "A religious message should be non-sectarian and non-denominational in appeal, interpreting religion at its highest, so that it may bring to the individual listener a realization of his responsibility to the organized church and to society. Speakers on NBC religious programs seek to comply with these ideals."[49]

Sarnoff, attending as an ex officio member, asked the council to review these policies because of recent controversial broadcasts, especially those of Father Coughlin. He was also concerned about listeners' aversion to sponsored programs featuring either controversial speakers and topics or commercial products whose mention on air might be unwelcome in the home. Discussion ensued as to the types of unacceptable programs, and Sarnoff asked to have a statement of National Association of Broadcasters (NAB) president Neville Miller on abuse of free speech presented to the council. That statement, issued December 22, 1938, commented on broadcasting of controversial issues by religious leaders and had received wide circulation in newspapers and the trade press.

Miller noted the influence radio had in American life and added radio "must be used in the public interest and not [be] subject to irresponsible abuse." In preserving freedom of speech, other rights, including freedom of religion, should not be violated. Broadcasters interpreted free speech on radio "as one requiring that equal opportunity be available for the expression of honest divergence of opinion." In administering this right via radio, Miller observed broadcasters realized radio reached all people, and consequently station operators had "no obligation to broadcast a speech which plays on religious bigotry, which stirs up religious or racial prejudice or hatred. Such a speech is an abuse of the privilege of free speech and unworthy of American radio." In addition, under current law broadcasters were responsible for libelous or slanderous statements uttered on their frequencies. In all, peaceful accord was key. "No obligation of free speech or of public service could justify broadcasters in allowing this great new social force to strike at the harmony of the nation." Inciting racial or religious hatred via radio were intolerable evils, and "in these troubled time throughout the world, there is a great need for national unity," he continued.[50]

Program content was a broadcaster's responsibility, and determining broadcasts in the public interest required mature judgment and informed decisions. A broadcaster was "well within his rights to demand an advanced [sic] copy of any proposed radio talk" and refusal to submit copies was grounds for closing facilities to any speaker. Speeches "plainly calculated or likely to stir up religious prejudice and strife" should be declined. "Such action is merely an act of good stewardship, distinctly in the public interest, and is not an abridgment of the right of free speech," Miller added and concluded, "The responsibility to accept or to reject broadcast material is one placed squarely on the shoulders of the American broadcaster. It is up to him to evaluate what is and what is not in the public interest. This responsibility the American people have delegated to him in his license to operate a radio station." The NAB would defend any broadcaster's implementation of this responsibility.[51]

The statement ignited a firestorm of pro and con opinions in the press and the halls of Congress, so Sarnoff suggested the Advisory Council hear other views from additional sources before deciding whether to endorse Miller's statement. To do so, he introduced Senator Burton Wheeler's critique of Miller's statement. Sarnoff believed Wheeler had misinterpreted Miller's views as "an abridgement of the right of free speech." He also presented the Hearst publications' view, endorsing Miller but pointing out this statement failed to mention "that the breach of inciting class hatred is equally an evil not to be tolerated." The Hearst publications' editors also believed un-American views, including those of Communists, should be forbidden. Sarnoff concluded with news stories on Socialist party leader and perennial presidential candidate Norman Thomas's views about radio coverage of controversial issues.[52]

In an article printed in *Newsdom* magazine December 31, 1938, Thomas stated he believed the solution to covering all controversial issues, including those raised by religious leaders such as Coughlin, was three-pronged. First, broadcast stations should be required to set aside time for discussion of public questions, ensuring that opposing views be fairly represented. Local and national advisory committees should assist in carrying out this provision. Second, no radio station, except during elections, should sell time on a commercial basis for discussion of controversial issues. Unfair advantages existed for those with deep pockets and those "demagogs [sic] who make passion and prejudice pay." Thomas thought it "unfair . . . to expect decent people to have to buy time to answer every attack that may be made." Third, stations should be exempt from prosecution for libel. Libel laws should be "more strictly applied against speakers and their backers." Thomas asserted that relieving stations from libel laws "would nullify the excuse sometime heard that programs were censored for fear of damage suit. Speakers and sponsors should be held directly responsible rather than the broadcasting station or network," he added. He believed libel laws should be extended "to cover the deliberate circulation of false statements or stories over the air, circulated to arouse popular hatred against any racial or religious group." While Thomas recognized the difficulty of framing such a law, he did not believe the country could risk stirring up "anti-Semitism of the Nazi pattern by the deliberate circulation of lies, calumnies, and forgeries."[53]

After Sarnoff concluded his review of Thomas's remarks, the council discussed allowing radio coverage of controversial issues in general. Francis Farrell cited the differences between free speech on radio and free speech in London's Hyde Park. He noted that the public could think denying Father Coughlin airtime would be an injustice. But Eleanor Belmont, who replaced Mary Sherman in 1936, said an "essential difference" existed between a radio program with its audience and a speaker with an audience in an open square. She added, "Anyone who wants to go to Hyde Park and listen may, but in England, the same people who want to speak in Hyde Park are not permitted a radio audience, which would without warning suddenly find itself a part of a discussion of controversial issues." Owen Young pointed out that radio's time limitations often precluded the equality found in a Hyde Park setting. Henry Sloane Coffin suggested that the program *Town Hall Meeting of the Air* take up the topic.[54]

Sarnoff then said that the major question was NBC selling time for discussion of controversial issues, religious or otherwise. From its beginning, Sarnoff noted, NBC did not sell time for such purposes, but he added the question now before the council was whether this policy should be continued or modified. Lohr pointed out that the FCC had oversight of the broadcaster's responsibility to serve the public, but in the final analysis broadcasters had to decide whether programming they carried was in the public interest. He added, "NBC has fortunately been guided in its judgment by the Advisory Council."[55]

Young then asked whether the other radio networks followed the same principles as NBC. Lohr noted that CBS "substantially followed NBC's policies but others did not regularly do so." Young summarized the two questions before the council: "Shall the rule be changed regarding religious broadcasts?" and "Shall the rules be changed regarding the sale of time to permit sale for controversial discussion?" Coffin moved and Farrell and Belmont seconded the motion that it was "the consensus of the Council that the rules on religious questions as they at present stand, are wise and should remain." The motion carried unanimously.[56]

Ada Comstock then moved, with a second from Belmont, that "NBC continue its policy of selling time for sale of certain goods and services and that it will not sell time for the discussion of controversial issues." As the council members discussed the motion, Belmont suggested reaffirming all policies previously adopted by the council and NBC, as well as those Lohr had summarized earlier in the meeting. Young asked that each point be taken up separately and "then finally, all reaffirmed by one resolution, if the Council so desired." As the first article had already been covered, Lohr then read articles 2 and 3.

In this connection, Lohr stated several instances in which NBC or a program's sponsor had allotted time for answering views expressed on the air. One was General Hugh Johnson's response to Senator Huey Long and Father Coughlin, and the other was Johnson's reply to attacks by F. L. Lundborg, author of *Sixty Families*. In the latter the sponsor gave time for reply, while NBC underwrote the former. Lohr then read articles 4 and 5. After discussion, Young called for a vote on the adoption of the principles to be reaffirmed as a whole. Green so moved, with Belmont seconding, and the motion carried unanimously. The reaffirmed policies were then retyped and distributed to the council members before they adjourned. The members also believed NBC officials should circulate these policies "whenever they deemed it wise."[57]

The following month, the council's secretary, James Angell, prepared a lengthy memo on the council's history for Sarnoff, which Sarnoff used to draft a booklet, released in March and titled *Brief History of the Advisory Council of the National Broadcasting Company with Digest of Its Important Actions . . . March 1, 1939*. The memo emphasized NBC's adoption of the council's suggestions in both programming and policy recommendations. Angell praised formation of the council's religious broadcast policies as "admirable."[58] Drafted by Morgan O'Brien, Julius Rosenwald, and Charles MacFarland in 1928, the policies held firmly through the 1940s.

Thus, under the council's guidelines, NBC presented programs from Protestant, Catholic, and Jewish sources. These talks and homilies were delivered by recognized leaders of the faiths, were nonsectarian in appeal, and were presented with the widest possible audience appeal. NBC's executives considered attacks by one religion on others intolerable, and coverage of religious topics was as nondivisive as possible. As radio evolved in the

1930s, however, religious demagogues such as Father Charles Coughlin developed programs that, while originally religious and benign in nature, became more and more contentious over the decade.

Coughlin's sermons and others' disruptive speeches incensed radio executives, including those at NBC, who did not wish to outrage their audiences. Executives sought to present programming most audience members would perceive as enlightening and instructive, and any contentiousness within shows only brought them headaches. Controversial issues and their coverage grew more significant as the 1930s progressed, beginning with coverage of the birth control movement in 1930. Overall, broadcasters wanted innocuous fare, programs considered unobjectionable and safe, which the birth control movement was not.

The Council and Radio Coverage
of Birth Control

IN THE LATE 1920s AND EARLY 1930s, sexual topics, including straight-forward references to reproduction, were absolutely taboo subjects for discussion in polite society. But sexual liberation, especially of women, seemed everywhere—in the advertisements of the day and the "flaming youth," flappers, and speakeasies that elders feared were symbols of the moral decay of American society. Such worries reflected an overriding concern within the dominant social classes of the time, including fear for the nation's future because of declining birth rates among white, native-born middle-class citizens and the growing population of lower classes, especially the immigrant ethnic poor and people of color. When society coupled this apparent social decline with increasing foreign immigration, "old stock" white Americans feared the effects of cultural and ethnic diversity on the quality of American citizenship. At the same time, fears of the effects of change and loose moral standards were heightened with the organization of associations promoting contraception and their opening of birth control clinics.

Some proponents of birth control recognized the desire of many in society to preserve the dominant race and class order. Therefore, these advocates presented the debate over birth control within the context of how women's access to contraception would benefit society as a whole. Others, however, sought to promote birth control as a woman's basic right. The battle between these groups fractionalized the birth control movement and led to further controversy as both tried to get their messages on contraception out by any means possible, including radio. But in trying to secure airtime, birth control advocates met fierce opposition, especially from NBC.

This chapter is the story of how NBC framed the issue of contraception to keep the contentious issue off their networks' airwaves. Most other broadcasters followed NBC's lead, and the strategies they developed collectively became the underpinning for control of nondominant, controversial issues presented over radio. This narrative chronicles and analyzes the confluence of three concurrent movements: censorship policies for broadcast programs in the late 1920s and early 1930s, splits in feminist ranks over what women's rights should be publicly advocated, and general fears that women's power over their own lives would have a detrimental effect on patriarchy, family values, and traditional family structure.

Promoting Birth Control in the 1920s: Feminists Frame the Message

Virtually all women involved in the birth control movement of the 1920s and 1930s were feminists, but within the feminist ranks, divisions occurred over how to promote the topic of birth control. Organizations such as the League of Women Voters, the National Woman's Party, and the Children's Bureau refused to endorse birth control publicly, even though their leaders privately approved contraception. These "social" or "welfare feminists," defined by scholar Carole McCann as those groups interested in social support programs that benefited women and children, generally saw birth control as a way to improve maternal and infant health.[1] In addition, they argued that supporting mothers, especially those from immigrant groups, in raising "good children" would result in "good citizens." But welfare feminists did not agree with more radical birth control advocates who defended a woman's right to complete sexual freedom. Such "sexual license was contrary to the Victorian ideology of feminine moral superiority upon which many women's rights advocates staked their political authority."[2] In short, welfare feminists saw any public endorsement of birth control as threatening their moral authority, which was built on ideals of female chastity and supposed moral superiority to men.

Welfare feminists framed their birth control message, first, in Malthusian terms of control over family size: Families should have only the number of children parents could support. If parents produced only the number of children they could nurture and educate, families would not become destitute and, therefore, would not be a burden on society. Second, they framed birth control in the context of "racial betterment," or eugenics. Today "eugenics" is linked to the Nazis' horrific practices in promoting the master race, but during the 1920s the term was tied to a perceived legitimate quest of improving society as a whole through scientific management of human reproduction. In addition, the terms "racial" and "race" were quite elastic during the 1920s and could reference nations or societies, in addition to specific ethnic groups. In essence, the 1920s phrase "racial betterment" meant the same as "social progress" does today. Proponents of many causes used both the term "eugenics" and the phrase "racial betterment" to promote sanitation, prenatal care, sex education, prevention of venereal disease, and pure milk for babies.[3]

In 1921 noted birth control advocate Margaret Sanger and her protégé, Frederick Blossom, formed the American Birth Control League (ABCL), the leading birth control organization in the late 1920s and the 1930s. The ABCL was the one birth control organization that "could claim national scope and hegemony." At its zenith in 1927, the ABCL had thirty-seven thousand dues-paying members from every state.[4] It lasted until 1938, when the ABCL joined the Birth Control Clinical Research Bureau (CRB) to form the Birth Control Federation of America.[5] In 1942 this federation became the Planned Parenthood Federation of America.[6]

Throughout the 1920s Sanger and the ABCL tried unsuccessfully to promote public support of birth control to the American public, as well as among other feminists and women's rights organizations, as a woman's right to sexual freedom. While many feminists of the 1920s promoted birth control in private, they believed the subject was too controversial and therefore inappropriate for public endorsement or widespread promotion. While advocating women's control over the number and spacing of their children, Sanger also supported contraception in terms of women's rights to sexual pleasure. More conservative feminists were shocked and thought this concept too radical and inimical to their feminist conceptualization of maternal virtue.[7] Therefore, within the ranks of birth control advocates, debate ensued over what aspects of birth control were appropriate to promote to the American public. These debates became part of the ABCL annual conventions. While newspapers covered these conferences, broadcast coverage of birth control proved difficult.

Radio's Coverage of Birth Control: An Overview

Stations were reluctant to cover any topic dealing with evolution and birth control, and station censors asked for and received advance copies of broadcast speeches on these and other topics. If objectionable material was found, the censors asked speakers to delete offending passages or words. In one situation, a station rejected an entire series of talks on child welfare because it included a discussion of illegitimacy under the title "Children Born Out of Wedlock." CBS barred any reference to "syphilis control" in a speech by Dr. Thomas Parran Jr., New York state commissioner of health. In protest

Parran resigned from the public health committee of the National Advisory Council on Radio in Education.[8]

Other broadcasters censored a speech on Malthusian economics by noted economist Gustav Peck in October 1930. The speech, "An Essay on the Principle of Population," contained references to food reserves, population growth and control, and persistent poverty in the world, and CBS cut the sentence "Thomas Robert Malthus, arguing against his father, made some startling remarks about human nature and especially the strength of the sex impulse, which led people to marry as soon as they were able." The company explained that it was not permitted to mention sex over the radio, because the talk was going into the homes of America.[9]

Signals coming uninvited into the home became the primary reason for "editing" radio speeches. In 1931, in his article "The Impending Radio War" for *Harper's Monthly Magazine,* James Rorty contended radio could never be as free as the soapbox or even newsprint, because of radio's intrusion into the home, and recounted a censorship incident he had personally experienced:

> In rehearsing a program of poetry for broadcasting over station WJZ, the writer was counseled by the program director to omit certain poems dealing with sex and religion on the entirely justifiable ground that to have broadcast those particular poems would have endangered the continuation of a valuable sustaining program. I accepted this censorship cheerfully. The same sort of thing happens all the time in relations with magazine editors and is nothing to get especially excited about.[10]

The American Birth Control League, however, did "get especially excited" about station and network censorship of its promotion of birth control. The most celebrated and public of these situations came with the ABCL's request for NBC network coverage of its 1929 three-day convention and subsequent debate of all sides of the birth control issue.

ABCL's Complaint to NBC'S Advisory Council

When NBC refused to carry the 1929 convention, the ABCL complained to the NBC Advisory Council. In its decision, the council had to determine for the first time whether information a group wanted to broadcast was in the public interest. The council had to reconcile concerns of traditionalist and modernist attitudes toward the contentious issue of birth control and, with its discussion, freedom of expression as it related to radio. In doing so, the Advisory Council defined parameters of free speech regarding a controversial issue of public importance. In the late 1920s and early 1930s, central to discussions of birth control were cultural as well as religious values.

As mentioned earlier, in 1928 NBC adopted five principles related to religious programming. In those guidelines tolerance and respect for what the council had recognized as "the three great religions—Protestantism, Catholicism, and Judaism—" was paramount. Messages were to be nonsectarian and nondenominational in nature and have the widest possible appeal. Broadcasts were to "not only aid in building up the personal and social life of the individual but also aid in popularizing religion and the church."[11] Carrying the ABCL's speeches would be contrary to these principles, as the three religions did not agree on the subject of birth control.

Joining the American Birth Control League in protest to the Advisory Council was the American Civil Liberties Union (ACLU). Forrest Bailey of the ACLU declared that as licensees using a public resource, radio stations were obligated to transmit all sides of controversial subjects of public importance.[12] The ACLU appealed NBC's decision on behalf of the American Birth Control League, first to NBC officials and then to both the Federal Radio Commission (FRC) and the NBC Advisory Council. In writing to John Elwood, vice president for NBC, the ACLU officials stated that "an objection to a particular broadcasting subject on the ground of its controversial character necessarily disregards the right of the public to be fully informed on all matters of public interest." The letter noted that New York newspapers covered the conference and questioned whether, in refusing coverage, NBC acted in the public's interest, convenience, or necessity as mandated in the 1927 radio act. The complaint concluded that in declining to broadcast the addresses of the conference, NBC "neglected the performance of a public service which it was under a sort of moral obligation to perform." The ACLU said it was improper for a public service organization such as NBC to censor material.[13] Copies of the correspondence were forwarded to members of the FRC and the NBC Advisory Council.[14]

The Radio Act of 1927 mandated that the FRC had control over radio, but the FRC wanted nothing more than to avoid the issue of program censorship. Frank Lovette, acting secretary of the FRC, wrote the ACLU's Harry Ward that the commission would act only on protests in affidavit form, which were made through oral testimony taken under oath. FRC chairman Ira Robinson also wrote Ward, stating that the commission's jurisdiction in the matter was limited, as it "extended only to individual broadcasting stations and (the Commission) has made no regulations with reference to chain broadcasting." He added that with the absence of a specific request to revoke the license of a broadcast station, the commission could take no action. A station was within its rights to refuse any type of broadcast material, so the matter was solely in the hands of NBC and its Advisory Council as far as the FRC was concerned. All council members received copies of the NBC-ACLU correspondence, and most acknowledged receipt, noting if NBC did not resolve the situation, they would review charges during the next council meeting.[15]

Only Owen Young, CEO of RCA and General Electric, parent companies of NBC, replied in depth to Ward's allegations of censorship. As chair of the Advisory Council, Young said he would bring the matter before the council "because it is certainly the object and ambition of the Broadcasting Company to use its facilities wisely and in the public interest." Young noted that among NBC's duties as a public trustee of broadcasting was an obligation to carry programs that listeners would welcome. These included both revenue-producing programs to defray broadcasting costs and sustaining programs offered as a public service. Classifying the ABCL in the latter category, Young noted that key in deciding what to carry was rendering "something welcome to the majority of listeners, otherwise the broadcasting station loses its audience, and its efforts, however well-intentioned, will be fruitless." He added more groups wanted sustaining time than was available and, consequently, programs had to be selected. Decisions were made "not in any spirit of censorship of materials, but in the conscientious exercise of judgment" as to how listeners would want facilities used.[16]

Young added that the birth control conference had been a competitor for the "scant sustaining time available" and that the "question before the Broadcasting Company was whether the interest of its listeners required that to be broadcast in preference to something else." He said that even though he was in sympathy with the League, NBC was correct in deciding not to broadcast the conference. Young wrote,

> I feel sure that a referendum vote of listeners would have demonstrated overwhelmingly that it was the kind of subject which was not yet ripe for introduction through the radio to the homes of America, available for any member of the family, of any age or condition, to turn on. The mass view may be wrong about this, but it merely means, if I am right, that your movement has not progressed far enough in public interest and good-will to warrant its broadcast by such a trustee of wave-lengths as the National Broadcasting Company.[17]

He added that NBC was under no obligation to cover any cause until listeners wanted to hear it. In other words, while the issue of birth control was controversial, it had not reached an acceptable level of public interest.

Young noted NBC carried other controversial subjects such as politics because the audience wanted to hear them. In such coverage, NBC selected broadcast times carefully so that an absolutely fair and full presentation of both parties' positions could be made. He added, even though NBC refused to air the League's speeches, other stations might be glad to carry the conference. He then invited Ward to lay the matter before the Advisory Council and to state his claim as to why the birth control conference was entitled to time "to the exclusion" of other public interest material.[18]

Ward responded that the ACLU was not interested in promoting birth control per se; it functioned to protect civil rights, especially freedom of thought and freedom of expression. He added, while the ACLU recognized NBC's responsibility in choosing what to air, the "feeling that the Conference program was of a character that made it unfit to be introduced into American homes . . . is based, we suspect, on a misapprehension." Conference discussions did not explain contraceptive methods, nor were they intended to promote the birth control movement. Instead, the conference presented scientific authorities on all sides of a "much misunderstood subject."[19] Ward compared NBC's lack of coverage with newspaper reports and asked, since the press also came into the American home and yet reported discussions fully, why did NBC adopt a different standard for radio?

Ward disagreed with Young's assessment that birth control issues had not progressed far enough in public awareness to warrant broadcast coverage. He noted opposition to the birth control movement made the issue controversial and that this controversy made the subject interesting and important. He said, "We cannot see the wisdom in a policy which holds away from the public all subject-matters except those about which there is no considerable difference of opinion. The tendency toward flat uniformity of public opinion under modern conditions is a thing to be deplored and resisted."[20]

Ward asked whether NBC's decision was made to please the anti-birth-control audience, contrary to claims that NBC did not censor as it selected material. "We gathered from the remarks of Mr. Elwood (NBC vice president) printed in the press that there was a body of public opinion opposed to the discussion of birth control which the company preferred not to antagonize," he wrote. "If this is true, we see in the rejection of the Conference program a form of virtual censorship. The fact that the section of the public to which favor was shown is respectable and strongly entrenched in its preconceptions does not alter the nature of the discrimination." In closing, he chided NBC for not risking disapproval of part of its audience.[21]

When the council met in January 1930, it reviewed the complaint and other correspondence. While published committee reports contain scant reference to the council's decision,[22] Owen Young's papers contain a detailed account, giving excellent perspective into how broadcast of controversial issues was perceived in radio's early years. Outlining the complete discussion and retained solely for later reference by the council's members, a four-page memo provides a confidential look at the council's handling of this issue of free speech and the public interest.[23]

NBC President Merlin Aylesworth began the meeting with a review of the letters and a November 19th public statement that explained NBC's reasons for rejecting the program. In part it read, "The subject of Birth Control is not only of a moral and a social nature, but it is of significance in the religious world. Propaganda for birth control is objectionable to a number of persons because of their religious faith. In this circumstance, the National Broadcasting Company does not feel that it should undertake the presentation of any material on this subject."[24]

To Ward's December 10 letter asking why NBC did not carry the conference addresses when newspapers did, Aylesworth replied radio differed from print in that the press could edit its material and report only those portions of a meeting that editors wanted. With radio, once NBC said it would offer complete coverage of a conference, its discretionary powers were gone; it carried the whole meeting, not just portions of it. He added, NBC "must, therefore, exercise discretion in deciding what programs are appropriate for transmission into the home."[25]

Charles Evans Hughes, soon to be nominated and confirmed as chief justice of the U.S. Supreme Court, began the discussion, stating that to him two kinds of broadcast programs existed: controversial ones and noncontroversial ones. NBC did not have to air a program just because a subject was controversial. On the contrary, he added, NBC had to be mindful of audience needs and desires and, consequently, to transmit primarily noncontroversial programs. Furthermore, controversial shows could be divided into two classes. The first class involved controversy for controversy's sake. Programs in this category usually pleased only those with special interest in the subject and might be unpalatable or offensive to larger audiences, he said, while the second type was exemplified by important political campaigns in which the public demanded presentation of both sides. To Hughes, NBC had to set policies to avoid the former and to encourage the latter.[26]

In applying this principle to the American Birth Control League controversy, Hughes classified birth control in the first category, as it had not reached a point where there was a general demand for its presentation. He added that if in five years such a demand existed, birth control might be an appropriate subject for broadcasting. When Charles MacFarland, chair of the council's religious programming subcommittee, asked how Hughes would respond to the question "Shall we give the public what it wants or what it ought to want?" Hughes suggested that broadcasters often do both, and in the "narrow field of controversy we must have the check of public demand lest we set ourselves up as a propagandist organization agitating for special interests."[27]

Elihu Root agreed with Hughes. He reasoned a vast number of people had ideas they considered of great value and wanted widely distributed. In time, some of these views would prevail, and the public would demand their dissemination. The criterion for presentation should be whether such a subject had reached a point where the public would regard its transmission as a service. When that point was reached, NBC would afford coverage.[28] To Root, discussion of birth control had not reached that point, and NBC had acted properly in not covering the conference.

The council's other members agreed with both men's assessments. Francis Farrell, chair of the agriculture subcommittee, noted that if the public had wanted to hear the conference, they would have protested in large numbers to NBC, and labor representative William Green said he believed NBC's officers made the correct decision. The only woman on the council, Mary Sherman, remained silent but joined the council's unanimous recommendation of making no change in NBC's policies.[29]

With this decision, the council's secretary, Everett Case, answered Ward's December 10 letter for the council. Access to the medium by groups espousing controversial views was different from that for the printed press, Case wrote, because radio came directly into the home. He then outlined the council's views, which paralleled statements by Root and Hughes. When a controversial subject reached the point of general public recognition that such a topic warranted coverage, radio would present the matter to the public as a public service. Until that point was reached—and it had not been reached in the controversy surrounding birth control—NBC would decline to broadcast the issue. Obviously, Case wrote, this principle's application was a matter of judgment. In this case the judgment of the Advisory Council was extraordinary because of the council's preeminent makeup. When NBC did decide to cover an issue, it would do so fairly, with the council's aid, so that all sides would be presented adequately.[30] For now, the matter was closed.

Letters exchanged on the council's birth control ruling, as well as the council's formal report, made the New York *Times* and other papers. They wrote that NBC had banned coverage because birth control was "a religious issue upon which the three great denominations did not agree." They carried Harry Ward's public reply, which reiterated his private letter, stating that NBC "neglected the performance of a public service which it was under a moral obligation to perform." Ward contended that controversial subjects needed airing, so that the public could form its opinions intelligently. Refusal to do so violated the mandate to public interest.[31]

Attempts to obtain airtime did not end with this decision. The Birth Control League approached 115 leading broadcast stations, including twenty-nine run by universities or colleges, to request time for either a speech or a debate on the broader aspects of family planning. Neither format would include information about contraception. To these requests, the League received two replies from stations saying that they would host either speakers or a debate. The Buffalo [New York] Broadcasting Company, consisting of four stations (WKBW, WGR, WMAK, and WKEN), agreed to use a series of four speakers already addressing the topic in Buffalo. In the other reply, the University of Minnesota agreed to host a student debate on birth control. CBS and four other stations also showed interest in the topic and asked to see speeches before coming to a decision. Other stations claimed that either their schedules were full for the next several months or that they were simply "not interested" in speeches on birth control.[32] In fact, during this time WEVD, a station operated by the American Socialist Party and named in honor of Eugene V. Debs, was the only station willing to air speeches on birth control without imposing conditions.[33]

Thus most stations took their cue from NBC in refusing to give or sell time to the American Birth Control League, as birth control was "objectionable to a great number of persons because of their religious faith. In this circumstance, the National Broadcasting Company does not feel it should undertake the presentation of any material on this subject."[34] NBC said that it was willing to enter controversy when the public demanded it, as in political campaigns, but no sufficient public demand for coverage of birth control was evident.

Leading discussion on NBC's refusal to cover the ABCL's convention were two elder statesmen of the 1920s, Charles Evans Hughes and Elihu Root. Hughes, born in 1862, and Root, born in 1845, had come of age during the Victorian years, when sex was an unmentionable topic in polite company and patriarchy dominated American homes. Both men recognized broadcasters' control over the medium, and both men reflected their times. Hughes's keen legal mind came up with a perspective on radio's coverage of contentious issues that separated controversial issues appropriate for broadcast from those that were not. Root reflected and embellished on Hughes's sentiments when he stated broadcast of divisive ideas rested on public demand for transmission of those views. When a controversial topic reached a point in the public consciousness that the public wanted to hear all sides of the issue, broadcast of that topic was appropriate. Until then, broadcasters did not have any obligation to cover the issue.

At first, it may seem surprising that the only woman on the council remained silent on so important an issue to women as birth control. But Mary Sherman could be classified, at best, as a welfare feminist, interested primarily in promoting women's rights in terms of female chastity, maternal virtue, supposed moral superiority to men, and women's position in American life as wife, mother, and homemaker. In this regard, she epitomized the split in feminists' ranks over what women's rights should be publicly advocated. In fact, even in private, Sherman typified the welfare feminist's perspective. After the council's meeting in 1933, Sherman wrote the Advisory Council's secretary, Everett Case, that she regretted she did not mention, during the meeting, the inestimable value of radio to women. In her letter, she said,

> I believe radio has benefited women, especially those in rural communities, more than any other class. It has lifted them up and out of the rut of housekeeping and given them a glimpse of the world outside the four walls of their homes. It has given them something helpful and vital to think about. It enables them to keep abreast of the times and sufficiently informed to be better companions for their children and husbands. In the management of their households they have been provided with a wealth of advice that they have always needed but never had before. In every way the radio has been a godsend to the women in every community.[35]

As seen in this letter, Sherman defined women in relationship to their husbands and children, as well as managers of their own households. Her position and views were consistent with the "women's club" mentality of the late nineteenth and early twentieth centuries, as well as the welfare feminists' views of women's power lying within the family structure. She and the other members of the Advisory Council would have seen women's power over their own lives as having a detrimental effect on patriarchy, family values, and the traditional family structure. This attitude was one that the other council members could undoubtedly endorse.

Fear of broadcast signals coming uninvited into the home was a major reason to exclude possibly objectionable material. This reason was, and still is, a major one for "editing" electronic media programming today. But many contentious issues, including birth control and reproductive rights, now receive far more coverage than similar issues did during the early days of radio. On the other hand, controversial political and public concerns have always garnered airtime and consideration. But, as the next chapter illustrates, airtime devoted to these topics came under question as broadcasters and candidates sought to use the new medium in political campaigns.

6

The Council and Controversial Political Broadcasts

WHEN RADIO WAS INTRODUCED IN THE 1920s, it began to affect the way candidates reached their constituents. No longer did listeners want to hear ninety-minute speeches—no longer did they want the shouting, gesticulating grandstanding common in nineteenth- and early-twentieth-century campaigns. Intimacy and equitable treatment of opposing candidates became the order of the day in radio's election coverage. During the 1924 campaign, broadcasters themselves set policy to treat candidates equitably. During the first convention of the National Association of Broadcasters (NAB) on October 11, 1923, the small group's primary goal was to deal with the American Society of Composers, Authors, and Publishers and issues of copyright in broadcast of songs, but they also debated whether politicians should be allowed to use broadcast facilities. The group decided to accept the suggestion of John Shepard III of WNAC that a political party applying for airtime be required to bring a speaker from the opposing party and that both be given equal time on the same program.[1] In that way access to the airwaves could be fairly distributed for political coverage, and the public would not perceive broadcasters as playing favorites. Thus the NAB suggested that all viable candidates be treated equitably, and notes from the organization's meeting in 1925 suggest NAB members followed this policy in the 1924 campaign.[2]

But as the campaign approached, concerns about "un-American" candidates vexed broadcasters. "Suppose a socialist wants to talk over the radio," one broadcaster complained to a reporter for *Colliers*, a popular mass circulation magazine. "What can I say to him, if he's a legitimate candidate? But, if I

76

let him talk, what will happen to me and my business?"[3] Eventually, assessing charges for airtime became the means for controlling access to the medium by undesirable candidates. Mainstream parties could afford time, while fringe parties could not, but the public and politicians would perceive that broadcasters were treating all candidates equitably, because all were charged the same price for time. No one could complain about discrimination if they were offered, but could not afford, time. Broadcasters readily adopted these policies, which were diligently followed in subsequent campaigns.

While broadcasters' policies such as these would probably have led to a quasi–equal opportunities doctrine being implemented on an industry level, a turn of events in the 1926 primary election led to the inclusion of a mandated equal opportunities doctrine in the Radio Act of 1927. During discussions about what was to become the Radio Act of 1927, legislators debated provisions regarding nondiscrimination by radio stations toward all candidates and other speakers as well. In their testimony on the proposed legislation, broadcasters noted that they engaged in "editing" speeches if material could potentially offend the public or if it were slanderous or seditious. To do so, they asked for speeches in advance, and it was one such request that led directly to the inclusion of Section 18, the equal opportunities doctrine (today's Section 315), in the Radio Act.

In March 1926, Cincinnati station WLW requested a copy of a speech Republican Senator James Watson was to give to his home state of Indiana on the eve of its primary election. Watson refused. WLW said that its policy of review was consistent with the radio policies then established by radio's regulator, Herbert Hoover, Secretary of Commerce. Though erroneous, this statement infuriated Watson. As chairman of the Senate Interstate Commerce Committee, he had oversight of the Senate radio bill then under consideration. In addition, he was a potential presidential candidate in 1928 and an arch political rival of Herbert Hoover, another potential nominee. Watson charged Hoover with setting the review policies of broadcasters and labeled Hoover the "czar" of radio. He described WLW's action as "censorship" and introduced provisions in radio bills then before Congress for nondiscrimination, or equal opportunities, in airing speeches of political candidates and for a commission to regulate the medium.[4] Until this episode, Congress had not even discussed an equal opportunity clause.

Senator Burton Wheeler of Montana, the Progressive Party's candidate for vice president in 1924, wrote an American Civil Liberties Union representative, Isabelle Kendig, that Watson was "furious" with WLW's censorship and now favored the passage of the radio bill with an amendment protecting political candidates from censorship. Wheeler added that the issue of the equitable treatment of speakers by radio station owners was brought vividly to the attention of Congress by WLW's request to review the Watson speech prior to broadcast. He stated that as chairman of the Senate Interstate Commerce Committee, Watson would work to move the bill, as amended, through Congress,[5] which he did. From 1928 on, the law mandated equal opportunity for all political candidates.

The Council and the Presidential Election of 1928

During its second meeting, in March 1928, the Advisory Council reviewed NBC's plans for the upcoming election, in addition to developing procedures for selecting religious programming and planning programs aimed at farmers and those living in rural areas. Mary Sherman then presented a proposal from the League of Women Voters to use radio for political education. From March until the November election, the League would present a wide variety of speakers and topics of interest to both men and women. Talks would deal with not only issues but also lawmaking and the "how" of political campaigns, including "How Congress Works," "How We Nominate Our Presidents," and "What Congress Is Doing."[6]

Such programs would work well over NBC's ever expanding network, NBC president Merlin Aylesworth noted. NBC had invested more than $3.5 million in broadcast equipment and was operating at a loss of five hundred thousand dollars for the first fourteen months of its existence. He added, "We have kept faith with our great audience and have provided only those programs which we would accept without question in our own homes." He continued, "The officers of the Company are fully aware of the responsibility of the Company to the public for clean entertainment, religious, political and educational programs. . . . We have encouraged the discussion of controversial subjects whenever they prove to be of importance to the public, and both sides have the opportunity to be heard."[7]

Aylesworth then outlined NBC's plans and policies for the upcoming election. NBC would deal only with national politics and national committees, as its officers believed local stations could best cover local politics. Both Republican and Democratic conventions were to be carried, and sponsors of programs that the conventions would preempt had not only relinquished their time but in many cases had agreed to sustain, or help pay for, the broadcasts. Both major parties were to be allotted an equal amount of time for campaign broadcasting on equal payment terms. Even if one party was richer than the other and could buy more time, equality was to be maintained. As for third parties, Aylesworth added, "Any third party which reaches any considerable dimensions on a national scale will receive equitable treatment."[8] In complying with Section 18's equal opportunities provisions, many of NBC's broadcast policies at this time centered on costs for time. Equity for the two major parties was to be maintained as plans for coverage of the conventions, campaigns, and elections evolved.

Candidates would pay for other time used on NBC and were expected to purchase the time well in advance for scheduling purposes.[9] The political campaigns were a lifesaver for smaller, struggling stations, as such monies supplied a large portion of their yearly income for 1928. In Chicago, for example, the going rate for airtime was $360 per hour. While some candidates deemed this price exorbitant, others considered pooling resources with three or four opponents, buying one hour and dividing time among themselves. One candidate bought time on election eve so that he could "scotch any eleventh hour canards or whispering campaigns which might be started in the last minute, and which would be otherwise difficult to correct."[10]

When convention coverage began, NBC's networks boasted more than forty affiliates, with more than five hundred persons, including 375 engineers, aiding in coverage of both conventions. NBC veteran announcer Graham McNamee provided commentary, peppered with quips provided by humorist Will Rogers.[11] In setting up coverage for 1928, NBC studied difficulties and successes of the 1924 and 1926 campaigns. It estimated nearly eight million receiving sets were being used, twice those existing in 1924. Speakers were coached for best radio voice presentations, as candidates knew delivery counted. Neither dull, flat speech nor flowery oratory was tolerated on the air. Strategists recognized that "in a closely and hotly waged contest it is possible that the man with the best radio personality might win a nomination or election over a field of aspirants possessed of less power to sway through the microphone."[12] Senator Frank Willis of Ohio observed that listeners would not appreciate long-winded speeches and would rather "listen to brief, pithy statements as to the position of parties and candidates."[13]

Planners for both conventions took radio audiences into account. The Democratic convention keynote address was moved to nighttime to reach the largest possible audience, while Republicans covered a table with a soft piece of wallboard so the rap of the gavel would "sound right" over the air instead of its usual timbre of "someone breaking dishes."[14] Radio loudspeakers were set up in department stores and outside radio studios and shops. Women gave porch parties, with radio furnishing political entertainment, and hospital patients kept up with the conventions through headsets. Cleveland's baseball team even carried a portable set with it to monitor both gatherings. Not counting shortwave transmissions to Canada, Europe, and South America, NBC hooked up forty-two stations for the Republican convention and forty-four for the Democrats. NBC announcer McNamee noted that the "Republican Convention cost $1.07 per second to broadcast. The Democratic Convention cost $1.15 per second." Because the Democratic convention was again longer than the Republican, NBC absorbed costs of $105,000 for the Democrats and $75,000 for the Republicans.[15] For the election both the Republicans and the Democrats purchased time for speakers to campaign for the nominees, Republican Herbert Hoover and Democrat Al Smith. Political commentator Frank Kent noted that in 1928 both sides spent a total of $1.5 million, or twenty-five times the 1924 total of sixty thousand dollars.[16]

At the third meeting of the Advisory Council in late January 1929, council members discussed issues about broadcasting's relationship to politics and political propaganda raised during the 1928 campaign.[17] Because he could not attend the meeting, Owen Young left a message for the members, which Paul Cravath delivered:

> I need not remind the distinguished members of this Council of the psychological difference which the political speaker must take into account when he addresses not a closely packed and often hysterical mass meeting in an auditorium, but this vast invisible audience coolly sitting in judgment around the family fireside. This aspect of the question is apparent to everyone. But let us consider the effect upon those sections of the country where, through habit or convention, one or the other of the great political parties has had a practical monopoly of the political stage. In some cases the rival party has virtually never had a hearing. It is the radio which evens the scales, which assures a fair hearing to both sides. Who can say what radio may not accomplish in destroying sectionalism and creating a new national unity.[18]

Young added that many difficulties existed in selecting speakers and programs to meet an expected public service obligation. "There is a complicated question of how to maintain the freedom of the air while assuring a standard of program which will be universally acceptable to our homes. There is a question of our relationship with other services most immediately affected by radio, such as the press."[19]

In his report to the council, Aylesworth stressed the significant role NBC played in the presidential campaign. He noted, "In political broadcasting the first rule of the Company had been to make its facilities available with absolute impartiality to the principal parties." Letters from the Republican and Democratic national committees and the Socialist candidate Norman

Thomas were the best evidence that NBC had succeeded. Because of the public's interest in political topics, Aylesworth had tentatively agreed to place NBC's facilities in the hands of "impartial, unofficial committees of the two houses of Congress," so senators and representatives could address the radio audience on important public questions. The council wholeheartedly endorsed Aylesworth's actions, even though such congressional coverage did not materialize at this time. Aylesworth noted that in terms of radio's evolution during 1928, political broadcast program developments were second only to radio's programming that reached farmers and residents of rural areas.[20]

But, Aylesworth noted, the "one outstanding demonstration of the force of radio" was political programming. NBC carried the Democratic and Republican conventions, summaries of the conventions of the Socialist and Communist parties, campaigns sponsored (and paid for) by party organizations, the programs on public issues produced by the National League of Women Voters, and election returns furnished in cooperation with the Associated Press, United Press, and the International News Service. Letters from the Republican, Democratic, and Socialist candidates attested to these parties' satisfaction with coverage.[21]

The 1932 Presidential Campaign

By the 1932 campaign, the Great Depression was in full swing, and Americans' standard of living declined dramatically. Businesses cut wages, and in 1931 mortgage foreclosures were eight times higher than foreclosures two years earlier. Net income was halved, but not all classes were evenly affected. The poor and middle class suffered more, and their misery created a new radicalism, feared by those wanting to maintain the status quo and finding voice on radio in provocateurs such as Louisiana senator Huey Long, Father Charles Coughlin, and Reverend Francis Townsend.[22]

Americans falsely believed permanent prosperity had been achieved in the 1920s, because they saw business planning overcoming the ills that brought about past recessions. Government and business leaders thought their rational decision making had achieved an economic balance, but the system was far more conducive to excess than to protecting against it. Investors speculated in stocks and land as "sure things," and those bubbles finally burst in the fall of 1929. Throughout the early Depression years, fraudulent dealings on the London stock market, nations moving off the gold standard, troubles checking the flow of gold out of the United States, increases in interest rates, and investors pulling out of stocks hit stock markets negatively worldwide and shook public confidence. The bottom fell out of the U.S. market, and stocks' aggregate worth of $87 billion in 1929 plummeted to $18 billion by 1933.[23]

During the early 1930s, industrial production declined by 50 percent, national income dropped 40 percent, unemployment rose to 25 percent of the population, and farm prices dropped another 55 percent from lows of the 1920s.[24] In contrast, radio was one area of growth during these harsh years. Few listeners gave up their sets, and by 1938, more than 91 percent of urban homes and nearly 70 percent of rural homes had at least one radio.[25] Radio joined recovery efforts by deemphasizing economic plight and censoring speakers, including minor party candidates, who wanted to address economic recovery efforts that relied on more radical methods to correct public ills. While President Hoover remained active in combating the Depression, the public blamed him and his administration for economic misery. His image in the press shifted from one of a progressive activist to an inept presidential misfit.[26]

In 1930 Democrats took control of the House and were one senator shy of taking over the Senate. That election saw broadcasters become responsible for libelous statements politicians made over the air, an interpretation of the law that did not change until 1959.[27] In addition, station KVEP in Portland, Oregon, lost its licensee for allowing a political candidate to use what was deemed profane and indecent language, which had been banned in Section 29 of the Radio Act of 1927.[28] These decisions fueled broadcasters' fears that their licenses could be revoked for airing inappropriate material during the 1932 elections.

By then, about 17 million receivers existed, more than twice the number in 1928, and NBC added two more stations to its networks, bringing the number of its affiliates to eighty-seven. An estimated 90 percent of the nation's listeners could receive one or both of the NBC networks. Statisticians predicted that more than 68 million listeners would hear the conventions, and both Democrats and Republicans aimed to please listeners.[29]

For its seventh meeting in February 1933, council members received information on coverage of the 1932 conventions, campaigns, and election. Chicago was the site of both Democratic and Republican conventions. For their meeting, Democratic convention planners set up a huge platform with a smaller dais jutting out for speakers. At the rear and placed slightly above the main platform, four glass-encased radio booths had clear views of convention proceedings. NBC, CBS, and other broadcast stations occupied the carrels. Announcers in the booths had two microphones, one to use and the other for emergency backup, while engineers sat at control panels to cut in microphones scattered throughout the hall. The newly developed parabolic microphone was installed to carry voices from the floor, while regular mikes picked up the speakers' voices. Under the control booths were soundproof studios for use by political leaders and for interpretive talks by political commentators. Another wired system kept announcers and engineers in touch with each other. Through shortwave, foreign nations were expected to tune in. F. W. Wile and H. V. Kaltenborn were commentators for CBS, while William Hard provided observations over NBC. Estimated costs of CBS's coverage fell between one and two hundred thousand dollars.[30]

A corresponding setup had been made for the Republican convention almost two weeks earlier. In addition to lengthy coverage of the convention, including major speakers and the roll call votes, analysts for both CBS and NBC aired four fifteen-minute assessments during the day—one around nine in the morning eastern time, another after lunch, a third in the early evening, and the last around eleven P.M. eastern time.[31] After the conventions most letters from listeners indicated favorable reactions to convention coverage and praised the industry as a whole, while some complained that conventions had not been carried gavel to gavel. Censorship charges arose and were aimed especially at commentators, who were labeled prejudiced and hostile, while some announcers were faulted for halting, hesitating delivery.[32]

During the campaign, the two major political parties consumed vast quantities of airtime, with NBC receiving more than $1 million in revenue from political sources.[33] Costs were high enough for Democratic candidate Franklin Roosevelt to declare that "the largest single item in our budget is to buy time over the air."[34] Both Hoover and Roosevelt used radio to reach constituents, and of the two, Roosevelt had the more charismatic approach.[35]

To find the largest possible audience, many important speeches aired at ten P.M. eastern time so they would catch west coast residents at home. Hoover's notification ceremony was broadcast from ten to eleven P.M. specifically for this reason. Plans called for four or five broadcasts by Hoover, and former President Coolidge was expected to go on the air in support of Hoover.[36] Even though he could address audiences via radio, Hoover still preferred to swing around the country making speeches from auditoriums and railway car platforms. In October alone, Hoover made twenty-two speeches in fifteen hours to add "that personal touch."[37]

As broadcasters assessed radio's use during the campaign and election, they recognized politicians still had a lot to learn about using the medium effectively. Listeners complained that candidates' speeches of ninety minutes were too long. "Shorten them" was the command, and recommended time limits ran from fifteen to thirty minutes. Shorter speeches not only would hold the audience but would also save political parties money. Contending "the rights of the listeners are paramount, especially when great public questions are under discussion," the New York *Times* noted listeners protested "against the effrontery of the broadcasting companies in taking candidates off the air before they complete their addresses."[38]

Often candidates competed over the air with members of their own political parties, and last-minute arrangements for talks and speeches that ran over their scheduled airtimes vexed the networks. If speeches ran long, networks and stations dared not cut the speaker off for fear of insulting the candidate or of facing charges of partisanship or censorship. When favorite programs were canceled in favor of political discussions, listeners also reacted negatively. For example, when President Hoover overlapped the popular Ed Wynn program, NBC's station WEAF received eight hundred phone calls protesting the president's speech, while the NBC Red Network's sixty affiliates received a total of six thousand calls.[39]

Both NBC and CBS also complained that candidates' last-minute scrambling for airtime upset their election eve plans. The National Democratic Committee contracted for time from ten to eleven P.M. on all of the networks, a move that involved more than two hundred stations. The combined NBC Red and Blue networks cost the Democrats about $17,500 for their hour of time, while CBS charged between $8,000 and $10,000, depending on the number of transmitters in the network. The Republicans reserved ten to eleven P.M. on CBS and were expected to reserve time over NBC's networks. Republican plans were upset when President Hoover decided to go back to Palo Alto from St. Paul to vote. Republicans and broadcasters had hoped he would go to Washington, where radio facilities at the White House were easily accessible. Socialist presidential candidate Norman Thomas scheduled his last address over CBS at 9:15 P.M. election eve.[40]

Networks planned coverage of election returns from six P.M. eastern time until the last ballot was counted.[41] Because all political parties regarded the "last word" as crucial, each party planned a last, hour-long appeal to the voters the night before the election. Even the Socialist Party purchased a short time period on CBS flagship station WABC. For election coverage, William Hard and David Lawrence furnished commentary for NBC, while F. W. Wile and Edwin Hill supplied assessments for CBS. Between reports, networks fed musical programs, with local station cutaways for local election results. As reports intensified during the evening, networks gave returns priority.[42] Listeners heard Democrats capture both houses, and Democrat Franklin Roosevelt elected president.[43]

After the election, the *Christian Century* commented favorably on changes radio had brought to politics. No longer were nominating conventions needed, it contended, because radio gave candidates the needed publicity. The magazine also editorialized in favor of a "new type of oratory" delivered over radio that would contain a candidate's warmth and personality and that would put a premium on intelligence, not on organized yelling crowds of enthusiastic supporters.[44] A New York *Times* editorial also lauded radio coverage and broadcast of election returns and predicted as radio news grew, broadcasting would become more important.[45]

In his report to the Advisory Council for its seventh meeting in February 1933, NBC president Merlin Aylesworth summarized NBC's coverage of the 1932 election. He noted "the foremost national issues of the year—the political campaigns and the problems of business recovery and unemployment relief—were covered." Broadcasts of the Democratic, Republican, and Socialist national conventions of 1932 totaled more than fifty-seven hours, time valued at more than six hundred thousand dollars. Campaign addresses totaled more than eighty-nine hours. At the same time, other organizations, such as the League of Women Voters, the National Economy League, the Junior Chamber of Commerce, and the National Radio Forum offered numerous shows about politics and civic affairs. With the Associated Press, NBC presented listeners with complete elections results. Numerous other programs covered both international and national political and economic problems.[46] Alyesworth also noted that under a plan adopted July 1, 1932, affiliates now paid a flat fee for sustaining programs rather than a per-program fee. NBC's total income for 1932 was $29 million, most all from sponsors, but more than $1 million in revenue came from various political campaigns.[47] Council members unanimously applauded NBC's handling of the 1932 campaign and election coverage.

Preparations for the Election of 1936

After the 1932 election, the Roosevelt administration began using radio extensively to bypass negative print coverage. During his first year in office, FDR often held twice-weekly press conferences—one on Wednesday morning at ten and another on Friday afternoon at four. More than one hundred correspondents, including broadcasters, attended these conferences.[48] By Christmas 1934, FDR had made forty-one broadcasts—eighteen in 1933 and twenty-three in 1934—and Mrs. Eleanor Roosevelt had made a total of forty-five broadcasts since her husband became president—seventeen in 1933 and twenty-eight in 1934. Eighty-nine members of the House spoke a total of 172 times, while fifty-three senators spoke a total of 136 times.[49] Believing Roosevelt had used radio too often, his advisers persuaded him in fall 1934 to curtail his broadcasts. So Roosevelt chose to reserve his broadcasts for his "fireside chats" to the American people.[50] This decision followed the Democratic National Committee resolution nearly one year earlier to manage speeches administration leaders made over radio.[51]

Referring to the Roosevelt administration's widespread use of radio, Aylesworth told the Advisory Council members at their 1934 meeting that he had investigated charges that NBC "failed to provide opportunities to the opposition (to use radio) for full and free discussion of political issues." He noted that Republicans had used radio far more often than the Democrats had during the Hoover administration. He also told the council that NBC had offered time to the Republicans, but speakers had declined it. Many told him the time was "inopportune" for reply with their points of view.[52]

During the meeting William Green, who represented labor concerns on the council, stated that organized labor and workers appreciated coverage of issues of special interest to them. He added they also valued NBC's aid in interpreting the National Recovery Administration (NRA) codes and their implications, as well as presenting all sides to controversial questions. He noted labor "would stand for no legislation which threatened to interfere with such maintenance of free speech."[53] The council members discussed the issue of equitable coverage, and their reports lauded radio's contributions to democracy outlined in Aylesworth's report. "Never before has the national government been brought closer to the American people," the NBC president wrote of the 1932 presidential election. "This would not have been possible had it not been for the National Broadcasting Company's policy, approved by this Council, of seeking always the presentation by representative spokesmen of various points of view." By then, the average broadcast day of NBC affiliates included nearly twelve hours of NBC network shows, of which 77 percent were sustaining. Public affairs programs made up a lot of this time, as the Roosevelt administration and the officials of the NRA and the Agricultural Adjustment Administration sought to reach audiences via radio to outline policies to combat the growing Depression. These policies were also subject to discussion, debate, and roundtable exchange, with all sides being presented.[54]

The ninth meeting of the Advisory Council was held May 27, 1935, at NBC's headquarters. That morning Everett Case gave Young an internal memo outlining the possible points for discussion that Aylesworth would raise in his report on NBC's activities. These included freedom of the air and libel suits, the issue of selling time for propaganda, the question of propaganda in sponsored programs, the development of educational programs, and freedom of the air and good taste. On the question of propaganda, Case reminded Young that a potentially controversial issue had arisen with the request of the ACLU to cover the American Birth Control Conference in November. He reiterated Hughes's and Root's wording for the policy that NBC adopted in 1930. Their approach stated that an idea is first "spread to others by agitation . . . and organized propaganda." If it spreads enough and "becomes a matter of great public interest," it then "properly has claims upon the time of the broadcaster" but not before. Case also noted that Aylesworth's report quoted from a recent *Atlantic Monthly* article, which praised American broadcasting as superior to European in the cultivation of democracy, but conceded U.S. broadcasting was inferior in the cultivation of good taste. Case noted that the question "Is the American system incompatible with the development of good taste?" might lead to real discussion among council members.[55]

As the meeting began, Young noted that Mary Sherman had died as a result of an auto accident in October 1934. Other council members could not attend: Senator Root was ill, and Farrell was conducting commencement exercises at Kansas State College, while Hutchins was engaged in hearings at the Illinois state legislature on communist activities at the University of Chicago and other universities in Illinois. By unanimous vote, David Sarnoff and Merlin Aylesworth were added to the council as ex-officio members. Aylesworth reported on NBC's activities since the last meeting.[56]

Aylesworth stated NBC was following the December 1933 press-radio agreement, known today as the Biltmore Agreement, which put spot news on the air at definite intervals during the day with the tag "for a complete report, see your local newspaper." In addition, he noted that in January 1934 NBC set up a Continuity Acceptance Department to carry out its new policy regarding "propaganda" in sponsored programming. He told the council that NBC was unwilling to allow propaganda in speech, drama, or song in programs purchased by commercial sponsors. Aylesworth believed that "the use of sponsored time for such purposes would put radio's public responsibility on the auction block to be sold to the highest bidder." He said he had convinced sponsors that such use of their time would detract from advertising within the program. At a later point in the meeting, John Davis asked whether it was possible to rid radio of categorical imperatives in advertising, such as "Do this today!" or "Get a copy tomorrow!" Aylesworth replied such messages were being crowded out by "far more clever announcements" and that "good taste was being added to such announcements." But, of course, such commands continued to be problematic.[57]

Aylesworth also noted that speakers opposing the Roosevelt administration's actions "had taken courage," and a better program balance of varying views on administration policies had been achieved between supporters and opponents. During Roosevelt's first year, "it was difficult to get the Opposition to express its opinions on the air," Aylesworth noted. Now, Republicans and independents used a greater percentage of time than the Democrats had during the Hoover administration. To illustrate NBC's attempts at evenhandedness in covering political affairs, Aylesworth noted the "Johnson-Long-Coughlin" controversy. In a banquet speech NBC aired, General Hugh Johnson, head of the NRA, had attacked Senator Huey Long of Louisiana and Father Charles Coughlin for their antiadministration views. Because Johnson's speech was not profane or indecent, NBC did not cut him off, "realizing that it would be necessary to offer Senator Long and Father Coughlin an equal amount of time to answer." Both Long and Coughlin spoke over NBC within a week. "Then we gave General Johnson an opportunity to refute and so closed the controversy," Aylesworth said.[58]

In the discussion that followed, Newton Baker asked Aylesworth whether NBC had ever been sued for libel or slander for the speeches it aired. Aylesworth replied that while some speeches opened NBC and its affiliates to possible suits, no suits had been filed to date. John Davis asked whether the new Federal Communications Commission (FCC) had continued program policies of the defunct Federal Radio Commission, and Aylesworth replied that the FCC had not censored or applied pressure on NBC's program decisions. Aylesworth noted that political affairs coverage and news broadcasts in late broadcast hours "had assumed a new importance and popularity." But, he added, politics was not the only popular format—the *Amos 'n' Andy* program had received more than two million responses to an offer of a map of Weber City, their imaginary habitat. The discussion then turned to education and radio. Overall, the council members believed radio was making significant, valuable, even "astonishing" contributions to American life. Davis said the report of NBC's activities in 1934 and 1935 "showed the permanence and wisdom of this whole enterprise of American network broadcasting."[59]

At the beginning of the tenth council meeting on May 7, 1936, Young reported on the absent members: Root was at his summer home, Coffin was on the Pacific Coast, Hutchins was engaged in university business, Davis was in court, and Green was detained in Washington. Both Davis and Green had hoped to come to the meeting later in the day, but near the end of the meeting Young read a telegram from Green saying he was detained and could not leave D.C. The newly elected NBC president, Lenox Lohr, was then introduced, and he presented a printed report about NBC activities for 1935–36 to each member of the council. Mrs. August Belmont was unanimously approved as a new council member.[60]

A well-known philanthropist, Eleanor Robson Belmont was the first female director of the New York Metropolitan Opera and a founder of the Metropolitan Opera Guild in 1935. In her earlier years, she was a celebrated, gifted actress. George Bernard Shaw was so taken with her acting ability that he wrote *Major Barbara* with her in mind for the title role. Contractual obligations prevented her, however, from taking the role. Considered a "grand dame" of the arts in the 1930s, Belmont also worked tirelessly on behalf of the Red Cross and the Emergency Unemployment Relief Committee. Born in Ligan, Lancashire, England, on December 13, 1879, she was part of the third generation of well-known English actors who performed on both sides of the Atlantic. In 1910 she married millionaire widower August Belmont, a banker, owner of the Belmont horse racing stables, chairman of the Jockey Club, and founder of the Rapid Transit Subway Construction Company in New York. After his death in 1924, she devoted her life to charitable activities, as well as the Metropolitan Opera. Upon her death at age one hundred in 1979, the Opera's officials credited her with keeping the Met solvent through her ability to raise funds. Naturally, she joined Walter Damrosch in promoting NBC's cultural endeavors.

After the committee reports, which congratulated NBC for its overall programming, the council turned its attention to David Sarnoff's reports on the future of radio and "its associated arts," television and facsimile. A discussion followed regarding programs covering the upcoming election and political programming in general. Lohr read NBC's policies regarding political programming, which the Advisory Council had endorsed in earlier meetings. Lohr reiterated NBC's longstanding policies on groups wishing to purchase time to present views on public questions. NBC "offered time at no charge to such organizations with the understanding that time would likewise be offered to others to present opposite points of view." Under this guiding principle "the air was free to discuss all sides of every issue before the public." But this policy did not extend to dramatized political programs.[61]

In 1936 the Republicans wanted to use radio for what were called "documentary dramatizations" and allocated nearly $1 million for all political endeavors.[62] The Republican National Committee (RNC) produced four programs under the title *Liberty at the Crossroads* to dramatize their opposition to New Deal initiatives that the RNC believed were contrary to American ideals. These programs were the first attempt by a major political party to use broadcasting to attack an opponent through a sponsored program that was not a political speech. Hence, these half-hour shows could be dubbed the first negative-campaign "program-length commercials."

To give the networks a sample of what these dramatizations would entail, the RNC produced the first two acts of the first show, a total of about twenty-seven minutes. The committee then asked NBC and CBS executives to review the program for air. After doing so, the major networks refused to carry the programs or similar programming, as they deemed the shows contrary to the public interest. NBC and CBS stated such dramatizations violated their policies for equitable coverage of political issues. Because the Advisory Council approved NBC's actions, an overview of these programs and societal fears about their impact on unsuspecting voters provides context for the council's endorsement.

Liberty at the Crossroads:
The 1936 Campaign Begins with Controversy

The first show began with a sonorous, male voice announcing the program's title—*Liberty at the Crossroads*—followed by an upbeat, orchestral flourish of brass and percussion.[63] Then two male announcers began speaking, intoning their alternating lines in increasingly solemn, alarmed tones: "Which way is America heading? Which way lies liberty? Which way leads away from our great American traditions of work, production and thrift . . . away from economy in private and public life . . . and toward a staggering burden of debt . . . toward destructive and confiscatory taxes . . . toward inflation ?" Then *Crossroads* presented a series of often-quoted lines from the Declaration of Independence and the Constitution's Preamble, ending with an announcer ominously declaring, "[A]nything which threatens the liberty and prosperity of our future generations threatens the foundations of our very nation."

The program then reviewed the American ideals of liberty, thrift, and the work ethic in light of the New Deal. "What has the New Deal done with the public debt?" an announcer asked, and then took the listener back to the 1932 campaign as an impersonator of Franklin Roosevelt delivered FDR's calls for halting the deficit and pledges for having government live within its means through a sound fiscal budget. Over a discordant musical rendition of *America the Beautiful*, the announcer then described the 1934 and 1935 deficits of nearly $4 billion dollars. Then he warned, "For every dollar collected in taxes, the New Deal has spent one-dollar-and-95cents. Where does the extra 95-cents come from? It's being borrowed. It's being added to the public debt. The total direct debt of the federal government is now thirty-billion-534 million dollars. . . . This is your debt . . ."

To drive that point home, a short skit of a young couple planning to be married was presented with the joyous strains of the *Wedding March* playing in the background. The young couple—Mary Phoebe Jones and John Albert Smith—shyly came into the marriage license bureau. They answered the clerk's questions in filling out the usual forms—names, addresses, and so forth as strains of the *Wedding March* continued. But, the announcers asked, if the clerk were to pose questions that would have bearing on their future happiness, "the interrogations might sound something like this." Suddenly, the lyric background refrains from the *Wedding March* became more dissonant. The clerk then asked them about carrying the financial burden of an American family, whether they had any money, and whether all their bills were paid. Then he pointedly inquired, "What do you intend to do about the national debt?" The couple was puzzled, "National debt?" As the clerk explained, John and Mary and every other American were responsible for everything the government owed. The national debt was a lien on everything John and Mary owned and would earn or own in the future, and as individuals, they "will shoulder a debt of over one-thousand-17-dollars and 26-cents, and it's growing every day." The average growth was $240 per year for each family, an astronomical sum for those earning around twenty to twenty-five dollars per week. Eventually in the sketch, Mary and John began to question their financial ability to pay down the debt and get married. "It's a low down mean trick, loading us up with all that debt without even asking us," John laments as the *Wedding March* shifts into a harsh cacophony. The announcer concluded the sketch on a biblically based note: "And, the debt, like the sins of the father, shall be visited upon the children—aye, even unto the third and fourth generations."

This skit was followed by another, starring two brothers, John and Leslie—stereotypical country hayseeds, with John trying to persuade Leslie to follow the "modern way of racking up debt" instead of paying bills on time. After an upbeat musical introduction of *O Them Golden Slippers*, John told Leslie that "going in debt is fashionable." He added, "It's the new way of doing things. Spend more than you get," so just like the federal government, they needed to "spend their way to prosperity. That's the new law. That's the New Deal . . . new times . . . new ideas. All them ol' saws about 'pay yer debts' and 'a penny saved is a penny earned'—all that's got to go right overboard. They belong to the horse and buggy age." When Leslie objected that he didn't care what the government did and that he was going "to stick to what I know is right and proper. . . . I'm gonna try an' pay our debts," John warned him he is "getting mighty close to treason." When Leslie said he was going to go out and raise the money to pay their debts, John cautioned, "Sh-h-h-h. Whisper when you use that word. . . . You can't talk about 'raising' anything . . . that's almost as bad as paying yer debts.

... Don't you recollect what happened to Bert Lyman for raising twenty barrels of potatoes? ... Six months in jail." Leslie countered that Bert did not have a government permit to raise anything. "Have you got a government permit to raise money?" John asked. "Of course not," Leslie said, and John reminded him of another friend, Ed Winslow, who could not raise a crop without a permit. "One of them government agents come along and made him plow it under . . . ," John stated. With that statement, their argument cross-faded to strains of *O Them Golden Slippers*, and the original announcers returned with more statistics about the "the New Deal's wild orgy of spending." With government debt increasing by more than $7 million dollars each day, they warned, "It's your debt that's growing, taxpayers. . . . Think it over, taxpayers."

At this point in the program, the end of the first act, Thomas Sabin, director of radio for the RNC, addressed the audience directly, saying he hoped listeners liked the first act of "this new type of political broadcast," because he wanted them to do him a favor. If they liked the show, he asked they call their friends and family during the following musical interlude so they, too, could listen to the show's second act to learn some surprising facts about the New Deal's agricultural program. "Thank you for performing this patriotic duty" in calling your friends, he concluded. The John Philip Sousa march *Washington Post March* filled the next few minutes of time.

And so the show continued through its next act, which outlined the limits the RNC believed the New Deal had placed on agriculture, especially the "special processing regulations," or taxes, on meat and other produce. The provisions of these rules compelled farmers to destroy crops and livestock to force farm prices higher. In addition, taxes were placed on processing food. These were often passed along to the consumer, even though manufacturers were supposed to absorb these costs. As more than 40 percent of Americans still lived on farms and a significant number earned their living providing services to these farmers and other consumers, the sketches in the second act stressed the negative impact such taxes would have on farm production and support systems, as well as consumer prices.

Together, the two acts were nearly twenty-seven minutes in length and were composed principally of three- to four-minute slice-of-life vignettes illustrating the strong, destructive impact the New Deal would continue to have on individual American character and initiative and on American society as a whole if Roosevelt were reelected president. The program finished at the end of these two acts, but it was enough for the networks to decide not to run the series.[64]

NBC's and CBS's Reaction to *Liberty at the Crossroads*

After listening to these first two acts, both NBC and CBS told the RNC they would not air the shows because the programs violated their respective company policies regarding political programming. NBC president Lenox Lohr wrote RNC chairman Henry Fletcher that the program involved "the fictionalizing of important political issues now before the country." While NBC "sincerely strives to reflect the thought of the religious, political, social and cultural life of our country . . . , these presentations," he added, "would violate the policies upon which the National Broadcasting Company has based its service to the radio listening public. To accept such dramatic programs as you have offered could place the discussion of vital political and national issues on the basis of dramatic license, rather than upon a basis of responsibly stated fact or opinion." The company would, however, be happy to furnish the Republicans with time for their "responsible spokesmen on the public questions involved." He would also bring this decision to the attention of the NBC Advisory Council at its next meeting.[65]

At the same time, CBS reminded Fletcher of its policy not to sell time until after the party conventions for political broadcasts. Even then, under no conditions would CBS "allow dramatization of political issues if time is bought after the conventions." Reasons for doing so revolved around what CBS believed was its "duty as a public service to devote a proper amount of time to the discussion of political issues without charge." CBS added, "While we realize that no approach to the electorate is absolutely ideal, we believe American voters have long been trained to discriminate among the assertions of orators whereas we do not believe they could discriminate fairly among dramatizations, so that the turn of national issues might well depend on the skill of warring dramatists rather than on the merits of the issue debated." In addition, sale of time over an indefinite period would destroy program balance, which "we do not believe to be in the best interests of the public or of good broadcasting."[66]

The RNC naturally objected to both NBC's and CBS's refusals to give or to sell time for dramatizations before or after the conventions. The RNC questioned both networks' decision to carry two presidential speeches in early January that in its opinion were "in large part political talks of a candidate," not those of a president. They questioned the decision—"[W]as this (action) in the nature of a donation to a political party by the Radio Companies or by the Corporations sponsoring programs which were displaced by the President's speeches?" Either way, the RNC said, the decision was partisan in nature, and the Republicans should be given "an absolutely equal break" to airtime. In addition, so long as dramatic sketches were announced as such—"as is done in the presentation of commercial programs"—the RNC failed "to see any legitimate reason for your refusing them." Such appeals were no more "based on emotion, passion or prejudice" than the President's speeches made "in the light of the impassioned appeal to class prejudice." The RNC planned to release its letters to the press "in view of the public interest involved in this question of freedom of the air."[67]

CBS president William S. Paley countered that CBS had never denied the Republicans' request for time when asked, but in this situation the RNC had asked CBS "to assume in advance that an address by the President of the United States to the people of America and their Congress was a political speech and to set aside in advance of the delivery of that speech comparable time for a Republican answer." CBS refused to treat Roosevelt in any way other than as President of the United States and told the RNC to request time after the speech, when CBS would determine whether time was warranted because of the nature of the president's message.[68]

Paley said the American public expected the networks to use their editorial judgment in allocating time for political propaganda or publicity. Coverage of presidential speeches was not a contribution to the Democratic Party, as the RNC claimed, but rather were "a donation to the American public," done in the true sense of serving the public interest. Paley disagreed "flatly that dramatizations of the political issues are unobjectionable provided they are tagged as dramatizations. . . . Issues should be discussed intellectually by responsible and identified speakers and not fictionalized," because such broadcasts "would be injurious to the American public." CBS adopted the policy of not selling time for coverage and discussion of controversial public issues to keep such debate from being dominated by those with the most money.

This correspondence and the exchange between the networks and the RNC hit the newspapers in mid-January 1936.[69] A Washington *Post* editorial noted the seeming hypocrisy of the networks' arguments. "Instead of meeting the well-reasoned arguments of the radio executives with the unproven cry of 'unwarranted censorship,'" the editorial writer said, the RNC would have been wiser to point out the inconsistencies of the networks' actions and statements. While the networks stated "appeals to the electorate (on radio) should be intellectual and not based on emotion, passion or prejudice," the same executives had allowed carriage of emotional, partisan speeches by administration officials, especially Postmaster General James Farley. Farley had attacked businesses as "dominated by 'a small coterie of unprincipled brigands' and 'self-professed gangsters' who are 'bent on destruction.'" The editorial noted that "in the field of passion and emotions" Farley's references to the "privileged classes" were "noteworthy."[70]

The Council Considers *Liberty at the Crossroads*

Because of this newspaper coverage and NBC's appraisal sent them before their meeting, council members were well aware of the *Liberty at the Crossroads* decision before the council met in May 1936. At the beginning of the meeting, Lenox Lohr revisited the company's policies regarding political programming, which the council had endorsed in earlier meetings. Lohr reiterated NBC's longstanding policies regarding groups who wished to purchase time to present views on public questions. NBC "offered time at no charge to such organizations with the understanding that time would likewise be offered to others to present opposite points of view." Under this guiding principle "the air was free to discuss all sides of every issue before the public." But this policy did not extend to dramatized political programs. After a brief discussion the council voted unanimously to commend NBC's position.[71]

RCA president David Sarnoff then presented the council with an eight-point statement regarding conditions under which NBC would sell time to political parties in the current and future campaigns. First, NBC sought to present various sides of political issues on a strictly nonpartisan basis through straightforward statements of fact and opinion made by responsible spokespersons. NBC would "not accept political broadcasts in dramatized or fictionalized form." Second, NBC would accept contracts for political broadcast time only between the close of the conventions and the elections, but "they should first satisfy their present indebtedness to us." Third, official political parties would be billed on the basis of NBC's standard rate cards for time. Fourth, "if a political broadcast interferes with a commercial program the national committees will not only pay our standard charges for facilities but will also pay the out-of-pocket costs to the advertiser for the talent cancelled." Fifth, if the political parties employed an advertising agency, billing would be done through that agency and include the normal agency commission of 15 percent. Sixth, if the parties did not use an advertising agency, NBC would not allow the regular agency commission but would charge the full standard rate. Seventh, in coverage of statewide or local campaigns, NBC-owned and -operated stations could sell time to qualified candidates for both the general and primary elections. Last, requests for time for political broadcasts not covered by these points would be referred to NBC's Program Department in New York. The council members again gave their unanimous commendation of this policy.[72]

The council also unanimously approved NBC's new policy regarding the purchase of time by the Communist Party. That policy restated Section 315, the equal opportunities doctrine, of the Communications Act of 1934 and then added that time would be sold after candidates met the filing requirements and "assuming that the application for time is from a duly constituted political party recognized in the state and appearing on the official ballot." But NBC wanted it known that it "adheres to its well known and long established policy of not wishing to impose censorship upon political speeches but it will not permit the use of its facilities for any speeches which advocate the overthrow of our government by force and the company must protect itself against liability for sedition, libel and slander. Our facilities are available only on the condition that these provisions be complied with."[73] These policies extended to other political parties as well.

Epilogue: *Liberty at the Crossroads* and the 1936 Campaign

Even though the networks refused to carry *Liberty at the Crossroads*, the RNC did find an outlet for the shows over WGN in Chicago. Owned by the Chicago *Tribune*, WGN was a clear channel that could reach much of the continental United States at night. Along with two-thirds of the newspapers at the time, the Chicago *Tribune* opposed the Roosevelt administration. During the fall campaign, the paper reminded its readers of the days left "in which you can save your country."[74] Consequently, it is understandable that the *Tribune*'s executives encouraged WGN to carry four *Liberty* programs.

These shows aired on four consecutive Tuesdays, beginning on January 14 with the program NBC and CBS rejected. The other programs followed the same format. For instance, in the second program, one skit portrayed George Washington being offered the kingship of the United States, which he rejected. When his officers urged him to become "a dictator in this emergency," Washington replied, "There never was any man fit to set himself up as a dictator of a free people." After Washington, an actor portraying Abraham Lincoln attacked the Democrats' "dictatorship" through the president's words, concluding that "Government of the people, for the people and by the people, shall not perish from the earth."[75]

Then skits berated New Deal relief programs and the purported political abuses in their management. One skit set in Coffeyville, Kansas, reported that relief funds created twenty-seven hundred new jobs just before the 1934 elections. This political manipulation of funds, the skit alleged, cost Republican Harold McGugin the congressional election. Another skit starred the Stebbins brothers of Bucksport Point and concluded, in reference to New Deal "give-away programs," "Did ye ever hear of anyone votin' agin' Santy

Claus?" The show ended with an actor portraying President Woodrow Wilson saying, "I do not want to live under a philanthropy. . . . I want only to have right and justice prevail so far as I am concerned. Give me right and justice, and I will undertake to take care of myself."[76]

The third and fourth programs also used such skits, and the fourth assailed Roosevelt by illustrating how he had not fulfilled his 1932 campaign promises. In 1932 Roosevelt promised to cut government bureaucracy by one-quarter. Instead, the program showed, FDR had created at least fifty new bureaus that employed more than 150,000 and increased the federal deficit.[77]

How many listeners heard these programs over the clear-channel WGN is debatable, especially since it aired at the same time as the top-rated *Ben Bernie Orchestra* program on NBC Blue and *N.T.G. Show Girl Revue* on NBC Red. Political speeches aired during the same month earned respectable audiences, according to a contemporary *Christian Science Monitor* report, but these audiences were not as great as those reached through entertainment programs. In one address Democrat Al Smith pulled in about 23 percent of the available audience, while Republican Senator Joseph Robinson's reply to Smith garnered 19.4 percent. While the report concluded listeners wanted entertainment, not political speeches, it also observed that radio was changing the face of American politics. Pleasant microphone voices and shorter speeches were necessities, and by far, the most pleasant voice belonged to Roosevelt.[78]

Radio's coverage of the 1936 presidential campaign followed patterns set by the summer's gavel-to-gavel coverage of the conventions. The Republicans outspent the Democrats over NBC, purchasing just over thirty-nine hours of airtime, compared with the Democrats' twenty-two hours, at prices up to fifty-two thousand dollars per hour. The Communists and Socialists each purchased one hour of time. One of the attention-getting stunts the Republicans tried to get on the air over CBS was a pseudo debate between Senator Vandenberg and phonograph records of Roosevelt's speeches. CBS decided that using recordings violated their ban on broadcast of phonograph records. But that gimmick was no match for Roosevelt's voice. "President Roosevelt is a magnificent radio speaker," one NBC executive noted and added, "no one matched his voice in the campaign."[79]

For Roosevelt's inaugural, now moved to January 20 instead of March 4, radio networks connected over three hundred stations to carry the festivities from eight thirty in the morning until four that afternoon. All regularly scheduled programs were canceled. Foreign rebroadcasts of the oath of office were expected to reach audiences totaling millions. Announcers were to be stationed in airplanes, the Capitol dome, and the Washington Monument, while others would use "portable" equipment to get interviews with celebrities attending the celebration. The Democrats even approved placing a microphone in the president's reviewing stand, and the American audience and millions overseas were treated to unparalleled coverage as Roosevelt began his second term.[80] Thus the presidential elections of 1932 and 1936 brought radio into the political arena, and later, as the world moved toward war, issues revolving around national defense and America's involvement in the war dominated discussions.

Controversial Issues of Public Importance

AS THE WORLD EDGED CLOSER TO WAR in the mid-to-late 1930s, radio programming became more diversified, and presentation of radio news and information shows became far more regular. As news and information formats expanded, issues of equitable treatment of controversial topics of public importance also intensified. Impartial coverage, of course, had been a concern for broadcasters, policy makers, and interested parties since radio's inception, but with radio sets in nearly 80 percent of American homes by 1938, just and unbiased treatment of issues became paramount. As previous chapters illustrate, the Advisory Council dealt with controversial issues, many of public importance, and as America seemed more and more likely to become involved in the growing war, reservations about radio's potential influence on audiences proliferated. Just how this new medium could influence and sway its listeners was *the* question, not only for governments but also for the radio industry, including NBC and members of its Advisory Council.

By the mid-1930s, program formats common today had evolved. From soap operas to prime-time dramas, comedies, and variety programs, American audiences could find information and entertainment to suit their needs. Music of all kinds made up about 40 percent of network radio time and as much as 50–60 percent of local radio schedules. Popular and semiclassical works dominated. Network musical programs were usually live, with artists and orchestras appearing in studios or being picked up on location via remote facilities, while local stations sometimes carried recorded music in addition to their live shows. Talks, speeches, and informative programs, including news and educational programming, comprised about 18 percent of network radio time. As the number of sets mushroomed and radio's popularity flourished, the information segment of radio programming came under scrutiny for balance in presentation of speakers and coverage of issues.[1]

The Council and Controversial Issues of Public Importance

The council held no meeting in 1937, and its last formal, published report was for the tenth meeting, held in 1936.[2] The eleventh meeting was held April 12, 1938, and by then, five members had died since the 1936 meeting: Elihu Root, Morgan O'Brien, Felix Warburg, Henry Robinson, and Newton Baker. No complaints had been sent to the council, but the members discussed a six-item agenda: broadcast coverage of controversial public issues, editorial supervision of programs, education by radio, children's programs, international shortwave broadcasting, and the social significance of television and facsimile.[3]

NBC president Lenox Lohr began the discussion about broadcast of controversial issues of public importance and editorial supervision of programs, noting both the difficulties such coverage presented in terms of fairness and the fact that no policies covering all broadcasters had evolved. NBC, he noted, had strict rules. Lohr defined controversial issues of public importance "as questions of nationwide importance upon which one group have definitely stated views, a second group have opposed views, and frequently a third group may appear which do not agree with either." He said, "People want to hear these views," and he added, "our policy is to give equal opportunity to both sides (or where there are more than two) as many sides as there are," because "freedom of the air differs from freedom of the press." Radio had no editorial voice, whereas newspapers could publish their own editorial columns, as well as editorialize within news columns. With radio, freedom of speech "has come to be thought of as the right to say anything you wish—barring the utterance of treason." Radio could not accommodate all the groups and individuals who would want to present their views on the air. Too many existed. Therefore, to Lohr, "freedom of speech on the air exists as freedom to express opposite views at approximately the same time or at the same relative time on the same network on a later date."[4]

In addition, NBC underwrote this coverage. Lohr said, "If we allow controversial subjects to be sponsored, money would control [the discussion,] for one side might have means, [and] the other none." Consequently, all controversial subjects were carried in sustaining time. But, he noted, news commentators sometimes drifted into controversy, and when they did editorialize, Lohr said NBC would "give equal sustaining time to answer that view." With this policy, however, affiliates might not accept the program that answered the commentator's remarks. "It is almost impossible to present an equal number of stations," he said, because of "variations existing in sustaining time."[5]

If editorializing occurred in sponsored programs, NBC could legally take the program off the air, but the company had never taken such action. When, on the rare occasion editorializing happened, NBC asked the sponsor to relinquish time for reply. For instance, when National Recovery Administration (NRA) head General Hugh S. Johnson attacked statements contained in F. L Lundborg's book *The Sixty Families* on a sponsored show, the sponsor, at NBC's request, gave time the next week to Lundborg to answer the criticism.[6]

The real question was what to do with controversial *discussion* when it occurred on a sponsored program, Lohr added. As Francis Farrell noted, sponsored programs with news commentators had changed the landscape of radio programming. Editorializing or presentation of controversial issues could take place in these commentaries. Council member Ada Comstock asked what would happen if a sponsor refused to give time for an answer to controversial issues raised on a program. Ada Comstock was president of Radcliffe College when she became a member of the council. Born in 1876, Comstock completed high school at age fifteen and went to college at the University of Minnesota and Smith College. After completing graduate school at Moorhead State Normal School and Columbia University, she returned to the University of Minnesota to each and later became the university's first dean of women. In 1912 she returned to Smith as the first dean of the college. She became Radcliffe's first full-time president in 1923. After she left the presidency two decades later, Comstock continued working to advance higher education for women until her death at age ninety-seven.

Lohr said NBC "could . . . actually commandeer the time." But, Owen Young asked, could this be done at the sponsor's expense? Lohr used a hypothetical example in answer. "If General Motors were having a strike and should attempt to use their time to influence public opinion on the subject, we would stop them from presenting such a case in time sold for advertising a product," he said. "A distinction exists between a sponsored broadcast for advertising and a commentator, who is presenting views on current views. The Company now decides." To Young and the rest of the council, this approach was appropriate, especially since current contracts could be interpreted to support this type of action. Lohr noted contracts prohibited coverage of "borderline" topics such as birth control and social disease, which might offend public taste if presented over the air.[7]

Council members agreed that NBC should have great latitude in any action it took. They endorsed the continuation of the policy that sustaining time be used to answer questions of controversy and that this policy be extended to commercial time, "provided it could be done in the time of the sponsor." Details of such a plan would be left to NBC's officers. The council members, especially Henry Sloane Coffin, believed "biased programs," in addition to those covering controversial issues, should be included under any policy. Coffin was president of the Union Theological Seminary when he was appointed to the council to represent Protestants. He began his theological career as a lecturer at the Seminary in 1904 and pastor at the Madison Avenue Presbyterian Church in New York City in 1905. From 1943 to 1944 he was moderator of the General Assembly of the Presbyterian Church in the USA. NBC's officers agreed, and even though he was not an official member of the council, Sarnoff added that "the rule would be stretched to the maximum" and in some cases implementation would be "difficult to pose without invoking censorship."[8]

While advance copy was usually required of commentators and others, "editing" the copy could be problematic. Lohr stated NBC often would ask a commentator to sign an indemnity clause to protect the company from libel, if the speech contained an attack on another individual. That request had, at times, led to the removal of offending passages. He cited an example of a speech by Secretary of Interior Harold Ickes that contained an attack on automaker and industrialist Henry Ford. Rather than asking the secretary to change his copy, NBC asked him to sign an indemnity clause. Ickes did, but when he spoke over the air, he also dropped the attack on Ford.[9]

Sarnoff then asked whether he could speak about recent developments in television and shortwave broadcasting. International shortwave had contributed to a propaganda war among different countries, especially the U.S.S.R., Germany, Italy, Great Britain, and Japan. The United States had tried to operate two shortwave systems, one domestically, the other for international purposes. Plans fell through when government officials realized everything aired would be seen as the official view of the government. A committee headed by the U.S. Commissioner of Education Dr. John W. Studebaker had been appointed to study the problem. NBC had its own shortwave system, but the FCC allowed no advertising of American products on it.[10]

Sarnoff emphasized that in the present unsettled world situation "radio is now an arm of the government." American radio was the most democratic in the world, he said, and no national problems existed, except those politicians caused when they wanted to expand or extend government control through regulations. As an example of the potential consequences of program censorship, he cited the December 1937 "Mae West incident" and the demands for government oversight and control. In this situation West, known for her suggestive performances, had appeared as Eve in an "Adam and Eve" sketch on the popular *Edgar Bergen and Charlie McCarthy Show*. Her risqué inflections in her dialogue with Adam and the Devil brought condemnation for being too racy and sexual in nature. While the Communications Act prohibited censorship, Sarnoff noted calls for censorship followed the incident and added that "the public interest, convenience and necessity clause has been stretched to control programs, sales of stations and of time." He added, "Mass communication is a new force. It is now through the ear, next it will be through the eye and ear. Any legislation seeking to control it would put radio in a straitjacket. To put, into the hands of government, control over the vast important medium of affecting public thought would be disastrous to our democracy."[11] Sarnoff called for increasing the license term from the current six months to several years. He also called for development of "definite rules of conduct for stations" and said all stations should abide by them. But he did not elaborate on what those rules should encompass. The commissioners on the FCC did not agree on issues and policy, so "the government lacked a well-defined policy on radio."[12]

As stated in chapter 4, before this meeting, Sarnoff and Lohr asked James Angell to oversee NBC's work with the council,[13] and the council affirmed its selection of Al Smith, the unsuccessful Democratic nominee for president in 1928, as a council member. NBC president Lohr then presented a statement of NBC company policies that the council had previously approved and asked the council for its reaffirmation of these principles on coverage of religious programs.[14] He then continued his statement with four other points covering controversial issues and their presentation on radio.

First, during election campaigns, NBC sold time to official representatives of the major political parties. It did not accept dramatizations of political issues because of possible misrepresentation and unfairness in the presentations. Second, in its sustaining programs, NBC gave equal representation to all sides of any controversial question "which materially affects the life or welfare of any substantial group." Lohr stressed "NBC has assumed an obligation *to the public* [emphasis in the original] to present the differing views so that the public may be fully informed on the subject." He noted NBC followed the same principle on sponsored programs and added, "In this case the sponsor may be required to yield time to a representative of the views opposed to the sponsor's speaker."

Third, Lohr said, "Freedom of the air is not to be construed as synonymous with freedom of the press or freedom of speech. Each form of bringing opinion to public notice has its own characteristics and limitations." Last of all, NBC did not censor or edit a speaker's remarks once an individual was granted airtime. NBC did, however, "check for violations of the law and for libelous, slanderous or seditious statements, as the courts have held broadcasters responsible for any damaging statement made over their facilities."[15] Council members heartily endorsed these principles.

Sarnoff then presented the report of NBC's International Division on the company's small, but growing, shortwave radio service. He noted annual expenditures were around one-quarter million dollars each year and "do not provide a financial return either on capital investment or upon annual operating costs." He emphasized, "This service is carried on in the national interest." He suggested that a private meeting of government officials and American shortwave, international broadcasters be held in Washington, D.C. "The national interest involved and the need for developing further plans which our government may not desire to publicize at this time to the rest of the world, would seem to indicate the advisability of convening such a meeting on a confidential basis," he added. "In this way, our government can obtain a comprehensive picture of the future as well as the present situation." While world nations were "now busy strengthening and increasing their physical equipment for national defense, to meet changing world conditions," Sarnoff noted mental, or psychological, preparedness was as necessary as physical preparedness. Of course, radio was best in achieving this type of awareness.[16]

Sarnoff then referred council members to his speech on November 14, 1938, before the FCC on self-regulation in the industry and said he would report any FCC action to the next meeting of the council. In his testimony Sarnoff had reminded the FCC of RCA's development nineteen years earlier and the service the corporation had rendered the United States in research, which benefited the entire radio industry. He mentioned the contributions to American society of NBC's outstanding sustaining programs, including the *Farm and Home Hour* and the *Music Appreciation Hour,* as well as the variety of programs found on the NBC Red and Blue networks. He added that "the record of network broadcasting in America proves the efforts that have been made here to safeguard public interest, to advance culture, and to provide unbiased news and wholesome entertainment" had been aided tremendously through NBC's own code of program policies. "[F]ormulated over a period of twelve years," he stated, "[i]t is based not only on our own operating experience but also on the wisdom and advice of the Advisory Council of NBC." He then called for development of self-regulatory policies to be solidified in a voluntary code of practices for all broadcasters, networks and stations alike. Self-regulation and "legitimate censorship by public opinion" were the answer to meeting the social obligations of radio and protecting traditional freedoms of speech and press.[17] The council accepted Sarnoff's report without further comment.

Dr. Angell then reported briefly on NBC's educational programs and called attention to the publication *NBC Presents*, a list of the network's public service programs. NBC's educational department activities had expanded since the last meeting and included new, regular broadcasts to schools in literature, science, health, social science, and music. Supplementary educational materials for these programs were available and would be mailed to council members. With that offer, the council adjourned "to meet subject to call" in the future.[18]

In his 1939 memorandum to Sarnoff on NBC programming, Angell reviewed many of the program proposals and suggestions made by council members. He praised broadcast policies covering labor's interests suggested by Green and musical programs for children championed by Damrosch. Less successful were educational program policies Alderman advocated at the same meeting. While many procedures had "in general . . . been closely adhered to in the succeeding years," failure to observe one suggestion—that educational programs be regular and frequent—"created a considerable part of the irritation" of educators. "The advantage of having it generally known that certain hours are educational hours is too obvious to require comment," Alderman had added in his 1928 report. He also called for educational programs to have the cooperation of teachers and to be adequately publicized.[19]

That programs had changed since 1928 was evident in one statement Angell made regarding Mary Sherman's 1928 comment that NBC "had within a very brief period of time raised the evening radio hours from the motley and mediocre to the brilliant programs for furnishing education and entertainment to millions of men and women every evening." He noted, "Whether she would have been equally enthusiastic if she had written in 1939, it is difficult to predict." Sherman had also cautioned against putting programs of interest exclusively to women in the evening hours, when men and children were likely to be home, and of course, that suggestion had been implemented.[20]

Angell noted coverage of controversial issues, "which has since figured so largely," was addressed in a policy statement adopted by the council and written under the guidance of Hughes, Root, and Young. He also mentioned that in 1930, Alderman suggested NBC create an office of education within the company. While this proposal was not fully realized until 1938, Angell said, the NBC Advisory Council worked extensively with the National Advisory Council on Radio in Education. In 1931 Green referred to the American Federation of Labor's plans to administer educational programming, but nothing ever came of this proposal. Angell noted numerous programs of educational interest to labor groups had been aired on NBC from then until 1939.[21]

In his review Angell suggested NBC develop a special "Division of Talks." Even though the council had not suggested such a department, Angell observed "it issues rather naturally from the types of programs considered by the Advisory Council." The Division of Talks would eliminate the large number of persons arranging talks, with the result of "somewhat inconsistent policies and very uneven quality in the performance" of the speakers.[22]

When Sarnoff wrote Young to tell him that NBC was developing a completely updated report of council activities from its inception, he also mentioned that he wanted to use the council to its maximum potential "to do a good job in the interest of the public as well as the Company (NBC)." To that end, Sarnoff suggested expanding the council with two new members, one to represent social and philanthropic organizations and the other to represent children's interests.[23] These members were not added, but Sarnoff used Angell's report for the March publication *Brief History of the Advisory Council of the National Broadcasting Company with Digest of its Important Actions . . . March 1, 1939.*

The *Brief History* included a list of all council members and a history of its formation. Summaries of its decisions on important programming issues included development of educational and cultural programs and coverage of religion and controversial issues, including birth control and the sale of time for propaganda, or commercial sponsors' presentation of partisan viewpoints. In its concluding paragraphs, the history mentioned the national defense issues raised in the latter years of the 1930s that would become all important in the 1940s.[24]

The council's consistent endorsement of nonadvocacy of positions and equitable treatment of all viewpoints resonated in FCC decisions in the early 1940s. In 1941 the FCC heard a challenge from Mayflower Broadcasting Corporation to the renewal of a broadcasting license for Boston station WAAB. In its decision the FCC decided "the broadcaster cannot be an advocate." In other words, the airwaves could not be used to promote a broadcaster's views.[25] At the time no broadcaster challenged what became known as the *Mayflower* decision, largely because broadcasters as a whole abhorred antagonizing their audience and their commercial sponsors. Later, in 1949 the FCC would reverse this decision in another pronouncement on editorializing that in essence allowed broadcasters to editorialize "insofar as it is exercised in conformity with the paramount right of the public to hear a reasonably balanced presentation of all responsible viewpoints on particular issues." This declaration was seen as giving broadcasters more of the First Amendment rights newspapers held and led to what later became called the Fairness Doctrine.

Preparing for War

After the 1939 council meeting NBC executives began reviewing policies "in view of the disturbing nature of present international occurrences and of the possibility of involvement of the United States should a general European war take place," and by April they had developed a confidential report titled "Broadcasting in Time of War." Overall, they found that radio would be an important factor in any future large-scale war. They noted, "Broadcasting has demonstrated its tremendous power as a social force, its appeal to the emotions as well as the intellect, its ability to sell ideas and philosophies as well as merchandise, and its capacity to reach millions simultaneously and to motivate them toward instant action." In the event of hostilities, the report noted, the United States could remain neutral, could offer economic and moral support, could become fully engaged militarily and economically, and could be invaded. Consequently, NBC thought broadcasting should be prepared to play its role in any of these scenarios, and the report addressed that role.[26]

If the United States remained neutral, NBC predicted, government censors would check all communications heard outside the country. "If broadcasting signals could not be heard beyond our boundaries," the report stated, "censorship would probably be limited to preventing stations from becoming propaganda media of warring foreign countries." To prevent incidents affecting American neutrality or use by agents of combatant nations, broadcasts of stations along the coast and high-power, clear-channel stations would undergo scrutiny, as they could be received at sea and in neighboring nations. NBC officials saw little change in this arrangement if U.S. participation remained at economic levels, although they believed government officials needed to "be prepared to broadcast to the American Public [*sic*] its reason for this course of action and report from time to time on the steps being taken."[27]

But if the United States became involved in war or even the threat of war, broadcasting would be invaluable. First, if war threatened, government officials should use broadcasts "to test public opinion and then inspire or suppress war spirit as well as guide the direction of our participation."

The report then warned that upon threat of war, it was doubtful that current peacetime policies for deciding what aired and who would broadcast would be sufficient in keeping "high emotional appeals" out of news and information conveyed to the public. Current policy for reporting foreign events included stationing "special event crews on the scene of unusual happenings, reporting the actions as they occur and bringing the participants to the microphone." These broadcasts reached "every town and farm in the United States." Imagine, the report noted, a broadcast containing "the crash of aerial bombs and falling buildings, the staccato bark of anti-aircraft guns, the shouts of searchlight crews, the sirens of fire engines and ambulances, and then—a shrieking mother with a mangled child, brought to the microphone, pleading for help for her country," especially if that woman spoke "in our own language, to tell of the chaos around her and suggest that we, too, might experience it in the near future." The report reasoned that "sound logic from strong and eloquent speakers might not stay the war hysteria that could easily follow." Consequently, policies needed to be set and precautions taken "to use the power of radio as an instrument of reason and not of emotion when, and if, a war crisis confronts us."[28]

If war did break out (or if the United States were invaded), all broadcast resources would back governmental needs and actions. "Broadcasters know well the powerful emotional force inherent in dramatic presentation, and have forbidden its use in political campaigns and on controversial public questions; but, in time of war, this restriction would undoubtedly be removed" and broadcasting would adapt to accomplishing war objectives. The report outlined how broadcasting could help recruit volunteers for the armed services, support a probable draft, instruct civilians in safety and conservation measures, assist organizations such as the Red Cross with war and disaster relief efforts, quell rumors through accurate news reporting, and mobilize the nation's people and economic resources to prosecute the war.[29]

Under all conditions, however, the report stressed, "*It is essential that the present form of commercial broadcasting be maintained*" (emphasis in original). To be most helpful in any war effort, broadcasting needed to "maintain its large potential audience and have it available for delivery when it is needed." Popular commercial programs held audiences, while national economic prosperity was enhanced by sale of advertised goods. But "perhaps most vital of all, civilian morale must be maintained by entertainment and diversion from the horrors of war." Governmental needs could be met without disrupting the present broadcast system.[30]

If radio were to meet its potential in any military crisis, the report warned, measures needed to be taken for war preparedness. Numerous questions needed to be answered: How much airtime, and what broadcast hours, should be reserved for broadcasts of information, instruction, propaganda, and news? Should these be network, local, or transcription (syndicated) programs? On which networks and stations? Who would be responsible "for information and propaganda programs—the government, patriotic societies, or the industry? Who will produce the shows? What about speakers, round-table discussions, dramatic presentations, sound effects and martial music?" After these questions were settled, scripts would be written, actors trained, rehearsals held, and broadcast facilities arranged. In other words, much needed to be done to ready broadcasters for their role in any hostilities.[31]

As for NBC itself, the network could alert and connect its affiliates in less than twenty seconds for important messages, reaching an estimated fifty million people simultaneously. Time schedules could be worked out to meet both government and advertiser needs, with commercial broadcasts canceled for emergency and special needs. Sustaining time could be given to the government without cost, but the network or another government or commercial entity would have to bear the cost of time NBC otherwise sold to bring in revenue. Who that would be remained to be determined. NBC also recognized that it needed to develop a plan in case its communications centers were sabotaged or destroyed. Citing AT&T's secret underground central control for emergency interconnection of major sea cable facilities, the report suggested NBC could create a similar backup program though use of high-powered broadcast stations and shortwave transmitters.[32]

Because network broadcasting was complex and because many of the principal executives were armed-forces reserve officers, the network was encouraged to consider its personnel carefully to prevent gaps in operation should hostilities begin. "Replacements should be provided," the report suggested, "for reserve officers in important posts who will be called to other duties." In addition, censorship boards and code or cipher experts should be assigned to prevent release of sensitive information such as troop movements. Guards should protect technical equipment such as master control rooms and transmitters from sabotage. Last of all, "on the threat of war, all broadcasting stations and networks should be required immediately to check on all their employees to determine their citizenship, military experience and the possibility of subversive activity."[33]

With the outbreak of war in Europe in September 1939, broadcasters began interrupting regularly scheduled programming for news bulletins related to the war. C. A. Spoul of the Aetna Life Insurance Company complained to Owen Young in June 1940 that NBC interrupted musical programs in the middle of pieces for war bulletins that could have waited until a natural break in the program occurred.[34] Young promised to bring the complaint to the attention of the Advisory Council at its next meeting.[35] In the meantime, he asked his secretary, Lillian Morrison, to ask for details of the incident. She found out that in this particular instance, the ship *Roosevelt* was bringing U.S. citizens back to the United States and had been the possible victim of a submarine attack. NBC had arranged to bring listeners the earliest reports from the ship as soon as contact could be made. "Sacrificing the music for the event" was NBC's guiding tenet in its decision to interrupt programs for news flashes as a part of its highly competitive business.[36]

In February 1941 the council met for what would be the last time and was asked to consider questions arising in connection with radio and national defense similar to those outlined in the confidential "Broadcasting in Time of War" report reviewed above in detail.[37] At this meeting, the council members were given a demonstration of television, updated on the ASCAP–Broadcast Music Incorporated (BMI) controversy over musical numbers and their performance (these two agencies were battling over use of music on radio, as ASCAP had demanded higher royalties for songs it licensed; in response, broadcasters had formed BMI as their own royalty organization), and informed of the latest FCC pronouncements on the NAB Broadcasting Code, with special reference to coverage of controversial issues, and the FCC's investigation of network monopoly and the potential resulting reorganization of NBC.[38]

They also talked about NBC's contributions to national defense, the main topic of the meeting. NBC president Niles Trammell presented an extended outline of NBC's activities and stressed NBC would present its normal schedule as much as possible. Among programs NBC had already presented were news programs about military recruitment and training camps and coverage of what Trammell called "acutely controversial issues, such as the Lease-Lend Bill." For reports on enlistment and related medical issues of individuals living in such close confinement in the camp barracks, Governor Al Smith stressed that the broadcasts "involve . . . medical officers in charge of cantonments." In connection with the overall national defense discussion, council members requested NBC send them materials on its public service activities and its advertisements related to national defense.[39]

Over lunch, Owen Young raised the question of the continuing usefulness of the council in light of the FCC's focus on public interest. Members believed that the council was extremely useful but should be called more frequently. Other members should also be added to reach the originally suggested, unofficial full quota of twenty-two members representing all facets of

American life. By informal vote, the council authorized Young to approach MIT president Karl T. Compton and the CEO of Libbey-Owens-Ford, John David Biggers, to ask them to join the council with the understanding that if they agreed to become members, an immediate recommendation for their acceptance would go to the NBC board of directors.[40] At this meeting the honorarium paid the council's members dropped from one thousand dollars per year to one hundred dollars per meeting attended, plus expenses.[41] This meeting was the council's last. U.S. involvement in World War II commenced the following December, and council members focused on other topics vital to winning the war.

Four years later, Owen Young wrote members of the council, noting he had submitted his resignation as chairman of the Advisory Council after he discussed the board's continuance with Trammell and other NBC officials. "I have done this because it has seemed to me that, while the Council was of very great value in the early years of network broadcasting, the major policies have now been fairly well established by the industry as a whole," he wrote and then invited members to do the same if they shared this sentiment. He added, "I am keenly aware of the obligation which the company feels for the service which has been rendered in the past by the Council, but I know that it reluctantly shares my views (on the Council's discontinuance.)"[42] Council members agreed with Young, and with little fanfare, the council was formally disbanded on April 6, 1945, at an NBC Board of Directors' meeting.[43] In a formal resolution, NBC's board of directors thanked the council members for their "unselfish and invaluable services rendered in the past to the Company."[44]

In part, Young wanted to resign because Edward Noble had asked him to join the board of directors for the new ABC network, which had been formed from the old NBC Blue assets. Young had told Noble he would not accept the invitation "until David [Sarnoff] had approved [Young's action], indeed not only approved but thought it affirmatively desirable" and concluded his note to Trammell by outlining Noble's proposal, saying "naturally I can have no deeper attachments than RCA and NBC—nor can they ever be created."[45] The 1932 consent decree, of course, had precluded Young from being a board member of NBC, but now that NBC Blue had spun off and was no longer RCA's property, Young was free to join the board of directors of the newly reorganized company, ABC. Trammell replied to Young that he was "delighted you are again going to interest yourself in broadcasting as I am certain it will be a big help to all of us . . . [and] if we can't have you, then I am glad the up and coming Blue Network [ABC] is to have the benefit of your counsel."[46] Young did not, however, join the board of directors of the newly reorganized ABC immediately, in part because of Sarnoff's dissatisfaction with his old mentor giving the new network the benefit of his expertise and understanding of the overall broadcast industry. Young finally joined ABC's board in 1948, never getting Sarnoff's absolute support.[47]

But when Young did resign from the council in early 1945, J. G. Harbord wrote Young, reminiscing, "I remember very well the afternoon at Poland Springs when you, General Tripp, and I discussed this matter [of forming a council], and I was in favor of the Council then, and I agree it was of value in the early years of network broadcasting."[48] He continued that the advice of council members was invaluable then for NBC, but that with the changes in the industry over the last twenty years plus the existence of federal regulation, the council had probably outlived its usefulness. While the council's demise was regrettable, it was understandable given these advances. Young concurred, and the NBC Advisory Council quietly passed into the pages of broadcast history. It had served NBC's initial objectives in giving the networks a means of deflecting criticism at their formation and by assisting NBC executives with program development and program policy formation. Both these purposes had been outlined in documents setting up NBC in 1926, and both functions had served the network well over the nearly two decades of the council's existence.

Epilogue

WHEN BROADCASTING BEGAN IN NOVEMBER 1920, no one could really predict how rapidly it would capture the American imagination and become a modern necessity. Over the next few decades, programming developed along lines today's broadcast and cable television viewers would readily recognize, and from 1920 to the mid-1930s program formats evolved that lent themselves to duplication. Programs adjusted to societal activities (and vice versa), and the networks dominated show formats that evolved for all times of the day. Quarter-hour serial daytime dramas broadcast at the same time Monday through Friday helped develop the concept of "stripping" and gave listeners a truly American genre known even then as "soap operas." Dubbed for the type of advertisers attracted to daytime dramas, the shows had slowly evolving plots that were perfect for listening as household chores were done. Weekly evening programs evolved into "prime time." These half-hour and hour-long shows attracted large audiences and were scheduled at the same time each week. They had permanent hosts or casts and recurring themes or formats. Expensive to produce, the prime-time shows came largely from networks or sponsoring advertising sources. According to the FCC, by 1938 network stations and their affiliates accounted for 98 percent of Americans' nighttime listening.[1]

For the most part, radio programming was not so much innovative as it was adaptive. At first, radio programs literally reproduced or imitated what had gone before on stage, on the movie screen, or in the concert hall. By the mid-1930s it was clear that these forms could be more effective if radio adapted them to suit the new medium. Special music and sound effects capitalized on the medium's intimacy and helped radio create imaginative pictures in its audiences' minds. Later, as demand for news and information increased, this immediacy allowed listener participation and "attendance" at evolving local, national, and world events.

As radio programs evolved, NBC's Advisory Council witnessed and endorsed many of these changes. That its founders, especially Owen Young, wanted the council to play a critical role in program formation and decision making can be seen in the honorarium of one thousand dollars that each council member received yearly for his or her service. In 1929 the per capita income was seven hundred dollars, and that figure declined during the Depression to a low of $373 in 1933. In 1941, when the council voted to reduce the stipend to its members to one hundred dollars per meeting plus expenses, the per capita income had recovered to $722.[2] With such a high remuneration NBC, and especially Young, saw the council as a "constructive agency" and wanted it to meet regularly as "a real committee of advice as to how we can make this radio broadcasting of the greatest service to the public, and how, on the other hand, we can avoid its misuse."[3] While the council met less frequently than Young might have wished, its members did suggest two programs that served the American public well—the *Farm and Home Hour* and the *Music Appreciation Hour*.

Admittedly, the council owed much of its origin to the likelihood that charges of monopoly would be leveled at NBC and its parent company, RCA, when NBC was formed. While the council did act initially to deflect such charges against the two networks NBC owned, another equally important reason for its founding was to provide NBC's executives with the collective wisdom of individuals who were well known but independent of any other ties to NBC or RCA. These leaders were established in their respective fields and recognized by society in general as principled, sincere citizens who would act in the public's interest. After its founding, NBC capitalized on the realization that the council's proposals and advice were beneficial to both the company's image and its bottom line.

Two programs council members suggested and promoted—the *Farm and Home Hour* and the *Music Appreciation Hour*—were carried on a sustaining basis as a public service to rural communities and school education programs, respectively. Both were successful, so much so that sponsors wanted to associate themselves with the programs, especially the *Farm and Home Hour*. No sponsorship occurred, however, until the late 1930s, when government participation in the program's production lessened and technological developments allowed targeting of specific sections of the country with products designed for the crops grown in those regions.

These programs were recommended during the council's first two years, a time when the council actually contributed both to NBC's programming and its program policy development. This period lasted until the mid-1930s when the company was well established, and the initial policies of the Federal Radio Commission succeeded in giving broadcasters a concrete delineation of acceptable program practices. Then the council's role shifted largely to one of reviewing and endorsing policies NBC's executives developed. At this point the public relations function of the council was also more apparent, and the press releases NBC wrote after each council meeting heralded the public service programming and mission of NBC's two networks, which the council had endorsed. Among the policies having long-term ramifications for both NBC and broadcasting at large were guidelines for coverage of religious programming and strategies and procedures for dealing with controversial issues unrelated to political campaigns.

The five principles for broadcast of religious programming developed in 1928 by the council's subcommittee on religious activities served NBC well. They allowed the network to keep contentious religious figures off the air and eventually were incorporated into other broadcast policies, most notably the 1930s revision of the National Association of Broadcasters code. That code, first developed in 1928, told broadcasters to pay close attention to their audiences' varied backgrounds to guard against offending anyone. The NAB code also built on the Advisory Council's conclusion that because radio came into the home, programmers should keep in mind that children and other sensitive groups were listening and program acceptance should reflect this reality. The code also emphasized radio's role in bettering living conditions and contributing to social good as a whole,[4] policies the council also endorsed. By the mid to late 1930s the NAB code's revisions reflected the NBC Advisory Council's pronouncements when the NAB specifically prohibited programs that attacked another's religion. The NAB code noted, "Rather it should be the purpose of the religious broadcast to promote the spiritual harmony and understanding of mankind and to administer broadly to the varied needs of the community."[5] This terminology echoed that found in the council's religious broadcasting statements.

Tied directly to religious programs in the early 1930s was the contentious issue of birth control. The policies the council developed in reaction to requests for coverage provided NBC with the means for keeping this controversial topic, as well as other troublesome issues, off the air. The two-pronged approach developed by Hughes and Root in determining public demand for coverage of a divisive issue allowed NBC to determine when and how it would cover controversial issues of public importance.

NBC would cover a topic only when sufficient public demand for coverage of an issue existed. Key to any decision to broadcast was NBC executives' verification that a sufficient number of listeners welcomed coverage. In the case of birth control, NBC and its Advisory Council decided that level had not been reached. Council members ascertained the birth control issue involved "controversy for controversy's sake," and the council deemed it of interest only to its promoters. The council noted NBC needed to avoid perceptions of agitating for special interests, such as birth control, so its executives should decide what specific controversial issues the network would cover. Otherwise the company would be seen as an advocate for one side of a contentious issue.

NBC also did not want to be perceived as taking sides in political contests. Consequently, it formulated rules for campaign coverage beginning in the mid-1920s. In 1933 those rules had clearly solidified to the point that when NBC president Merlin Aylesworth reported on NBC's coverage of the 1932 presidential election, Advisory Council members praised the company's equitable coverage and offered no suggestions for improvement. Four years later, when negative political skits aimed at an opponent became a focal point of the presidential campaign, the council unanimously approved NBC's policy of denying the Republican National Committee the right to purchase time for inappropriate or potentially deceptive political fare. NBC and CBS had reasoned the electorate could misconstrue such programs, even though they were obviously political in nature. The networks concluded any likely misleading programming was not in the public interest, so these skits should be banned from their airwaves.

The public could also judge such programs one-sided and therefore controversial. Broadcasters, including NBC, did not want the label of "partisan" or "biased" placed on their political programs, so they made a deliberate effort not to offend potential audiences by trying to present all sides of political campaigns and, by extension, coverage of controversial issues of public importance. Thus, by the late 1930s NBC had expanded its policies on controversial programming, begun with its denial of time to vitriolic religious speakers and the American Birth Control League, to other probable divisive topics. These more extensive policies mandated presentation of all sides of controversial issues.

These rules were strictly enforced after war erupted in Europe and speakers wanted airtime to discuss the pros and cons of topics such as America maintaining its neutrality. In 1940 and 1941, as the United States moved closer to involvement in World War II, NBC drew up plans summarizing its response to threats of war and actual involvement in a war. These procedures provided a blueprint for programming when the United States finally joined World War II.

After the war, broadcast coverage of controversial issues found voice in FCC policies that ultimately became the "Fairness Doctrine." This doctrine, upheld in the 1969 Supreme Court *Red Lion v. FCC* decision,[6] can be traced to the NBC Advisory Council's discussions of controversial issues and their carriage on NBC. Under the council's pronouncements NBC could avoid coverage of any controversial issues, but under the Fairness Doctrine broadcasters had an affirmative obligation to cover controversial issues of public importance. In other words broadcasters could not ignore public issues and concerns in their listening and viewing areas. They *had* to carry programming that addressed these topics and, in their programming, to give airtime to all viewpoints with a significant measure of support. This postwar policy completely reversed the council's directive to keep contentious public issues off the air, if they might offend audiences.

The Fairness Doctrine held until the FCC eliminated it in 1987 in a controversial decision that found "the fairness doctrine [*sic*] chills speech and is not narrowly tailored to achieve a substantial government interest." The FCC concluded that "the fairness doctrine [*sic*] contravenes the First Amendment and thereby disserves the public interest." The FCC would cease enforcement.[7] With its demise, talk radio began to take off, and today the environment is one in which Father Coughlin would feel right at home.

Coughlin would also be at home on many of today's cable talk or news channels that came from the expansion of cable in the 1970s and 1980s. This development, plus the advent of the Internet in the 1990s, continued to add voices to the media marketplace and to change the media landscape dramatically. More voices had diminished the perceived need for a Fairness Doctrine, and under the presidency of Ronald Reagan, government as a whole began to dismantle regulatory policies covering many industries, including broadcast and telecommunications. This climate allowed the FCC to abandon the doctrine, which the broadcast media welcomed with a collective sigh of relief, as cable had effectively begun to erode their monopoly on electronic information and entertainment.

In particular, broadcasters recognized cable could carry programming unsuitable for broadcast. Lower courts had recognized this capability in the early 1980s and specifically stated cable was not broadcasting and could not be regulated as such. Cable had been "invited to the home," so its non-broadcast channels could carry material deemed inappropriate, or even indecent, for broadcast.[8] Today, content regulation for cable is left largely in the hands of parents and parental controls (such as V-chip technology), as each household is expected to set its own standards for video consumption.[9] To date, the same parental control system seems to apply to Internet content.[10] While technology did not allow such supervision in the 1930s, the Advisory Council members would most likely have approved its use instead of content regulation. As review of their policies shows, the council's overall approach was business-oriented, and its members collectively saw network executives exercising their judgment to serve audiences in the public interest while at the same time serving the business interests of broadcasting.

The council's endorsement of NBC's policies for coverage of political candidates and campaigns also served broadcasting's interests in the 1930s, but this policy arena also changed dramatically with the widespread growth of television in the 1950s. After several claims for equal opportunity under Section 315 of the Communications Act resulted in FCC decisions stating any candidate appearance triggered the provision, Congress took action in 1959 and added four exemptions to the law. Exempt were appearances by legally qualified candidates in bona fide newscasts, bona fide news interview programs, bona fide news documentaries (if the appearance was incidental to the subject matter of the documentary), and on-the-spot coverage of bona fide news events.[11]

These exemptions, plus the 1959 Supreme Court decision known as the *WDAY* case, resolved problems for broadcasters in covering candidates during the television era. Before *WDAY*, broadcasters could be held legally responsible for defamatory statements candidates made. Consequently, radio and early television executives asked for advance copies of speeches so they could peruse them for potentially libelous or slanderous material. While most candidates complied willingly, others balked at such oversight, labeling it censorship.[12] In *WDAY* the Supreme Court unanimously held Section 315 prohibited broadcaster censorship of candidates. The court also held in a narrower five-to-four vote that Section 315 preempted state defamation law and created an absolute privilege that protected licenses, but not the candidates themselves, from liability for statements made.[13]

In 1971 Congress adopted the Federal Election Campaign Act and placed an additional control on broadcasters' oversight of candidate speech in Section 312 of the Communications Act, which dealt with broadcast license revocation. This new subsection stated the FCC could revoke a broadcast license for "willful or repeated failure to allow reasonable access" to broadcast facilities for candidates for federal office.[14] In 1980 cases began to reach the Supreme Court with issues focusing on when a campaign began and how requests for reasonable access should be made. The decision made in *CBS v. FCC*[15] altered the relationship between candidates and broadcasters. In this case, the committee seeking the reelection of President Jimmy Carter and Vice President Walter Mondale asked the broadcast networks for time in December 1979 to show a documentary on Carter's first term. Carter had just announced he was seeking renomination, and the committee wanted thirty minutes in prime time to kick off his campaign.

CBS proposed two five-minute segments, only one in prime time, while ABC said it would make time available in January 1980. NBC said it was "too early in the political season for nationwide broadcast time to be made available for political purposes." The Carter-Mondale committee complained to the FCC, which found the networks in violation of Section 312(a)(7). The court of appeals and the Supreme Court agreed, essentially saying candidates controlled their campaigns and decisions about when the campaign began and how it would be conducted were in the hands of the candidates, not the broadcasters. In this situation, if candidates wanted to begin campaigning nearly a year before the election, that was their decision. Broadcasters could not reject requests for time outright. This case and others helped shape today's prolonged presidential campaigns, whose protracted nature would astound and probably dismay members of NBC's Advisory Council.

The council would also be disappointed, but probably not surprised, by injurious elements in today's electronic media campaigns, especially campaign attack ads and negative political rhetoric. Used to seeing such assaults in print and speeches, the council genuinely had higher aspirations for the new medium; but as radio and later television became the chief means for receipt of news and information, these media understandably changed to bring audiences political programming candidates believed would help them win elections.

All in all, during the interwar years the NBC Advisory Council influenced the evolution of sustaining programs, program format development, and rules set to control controversial and political speech. Selected for their educational, career, and cultural experiences, the council members brought their collective wisdom to NBC's decision-making process. For the most part, these individuals held those mainstream values that dominated American society during the Roaring Twenties and the Depression, and their decisions about programming largely reflected more traditional, conservative beliefs. Often the council functioned as "a creature of NBC," as it reviewed policies and guidelines that actually promoted NBC's business by curbing what was considered then to be undesirable speech over radio.

At the same time, the council's guidance helped NBC plan programs in the public interest, which, as Owen Young noted at the first Advisory

Council meeting, "is the only way to serve the business interests of the founders of the plan [for the network]."[16] By the time the council dissolved at the end of World War II, it had fulfilled its twofold purpose: to advise NBC in its early years on programming and to deflect allegations of monopoly and censorship in the network's formation. As it quietly vanished into broadcast history in 1945, the council's members could look back with a certain amount of satisfaction on their influence over NBC's programming and policies and, by extension, on the development of electronic media in the United States.

NOTES

BIBLIOGRAPHY

INDEX

Notes

1. An Overview: The Evolution of RCA and Radio Programming

1. Harrison B. Summers and Worth McDougald, *Programming on Radio and Television*, 2nd ed. (Athens, GA: University of Georgia, 1959), 9–10; and Ray Barfield, *Listening to Radio, 1920–1950* (Westport, CN: Praeger, 1996), 62.

2. George H. Douglas, *The Early Days of Radio Broadcasting* (Jefferson, NC: McFarland, 1987), 23.

3. Norman Brokenshire, *This Is Norman Brokenshire* (New York: David McKay, 1954), 53–54. Also, see Douglas, *Early Days*, 63.

4. Douglas, *Early Days*, 25–32.

5. Hiram Jome, *Economics of the Radio Industry* (Chicago: A. W. Shaw, 1925), 175–76, and Summers and McDougald, *Programming on Radio*, 11.

6. Summers and McDougald, *Programming on Radio*, 9–12.

7. Erik Barnouw, *A Tower in Babel: A History of Broadcasting in the United States to 1933* (New York: Oxford University Press, 1966), 57–61; Gleason Archer, *History of Radio to 1926* (New York: American Historical Society, 1938), 176–90; and Josephine and Everett Case, *Owen D. Young and American Enterprise* (Boston: Godine, 1982), 171–91.

8. Owen D. Young to Admiral Bullard, letter, June 16, 1919; A. G. Davis to Owen Young, letter, April 10, 1919; Owen Young to Miles Poindexter, letter, November 11, 1919, Owen D. Young Papers (hereafter ODY Papers), box 193, Valuable Radio Papers, St. Lawrence University Libraries, Canton, New York; and A. G. Davis to Owen Young, letter, June 30, 1919, ODY Papers, box 75, Radio; and Case and Case, *Owen D. Young*, 173–76.

9. Case and Case, *Owen D. Young*, 174–80; Owen Young to Admiral Bullard, letter, June 16, 1919, and Owen Young to Josephus Daniels, letter, June 11, 1919, ODY Papers, box 193, Valuable Radio Papers; A. G. Davis to Young, letter,

August 5, 1919, and Young to Davis, cablegram, August 22, 1919, ODY papers, box 86, RCA.

10. Case and Case, *Owen D. Young*, 178–91; Owen Young to Miles Poindexter, letter, November 11, 1919, ODY Papers, box 193, Valuable Radio Papers.

11. Owen Young to Miles Poindexter, letter, November 11, 1919, ODY Papers, box 193, Valuable Radio Papers.

12. Barnouw, *Tower in Babel*, 57–74; Louise M. Benjamin, *Freedom of the Air and the Public Interest: First Amendment Rights in Broadcasting to 1935* (Carbondale: Southern Illinois University Press, 2001), 56; Philip Rosen, *Modern Stentors* (Westport, CN: Greenwood Press, 1980), 25–29; E. K. Hall and S. W. Fordyce, memo, "May 12, 1920, Washington," and Fordyce to Young, letter, May 20, 1920, ODY Papers, box 95, AT&T Wireless; and H. M. Daugherty to Sheffield, letter, August 25, 1921, AT&T Collection, box 50, RCA Agreements–1921, AT&T Archives.

13. Barnouw, *Tower in Babel*, 161–62; Benjamin, *Freedom of the Air*, 56.

14. Barnouw, *Tower in Babel*, 180–84; Benjamin, *Freedom of the Air*, 55–58.

15. Barnouw, *Tower in Babel*, 184–85; Benjamin, *Freedom of the Air*, 58–61.

16. E. B. Mallory and Henry Marschalk, Speeches before the Second Annual Radio Conference under the Auspices of the Music Master Corp. of Philadelphia, March 6, 1924, 22 and 38, Commerce Papers, box 389, Herbert Hoover Presidential Library; U.S. Congress, House, hearings before the Committee on the Merchant Marine and Fisheries on H.R. 7357, "To Regulate Radio Communication and for Other Purposes," 68th Congress, first session, 83; and Benjamin, *Freedom of the Air*, 37–53.

17. "The Use of Bell System Facilities in the Broadcasting of the Political Campaign of 1924," AT&T Collection, box 42, Radio Broadcasting–Bell System Activity—1922–23, 1925–26; and Benjamin, *Freedom of the Air*, 37–53.

18. Benjamin, *Freedom of the Air*, 39–41.

19. Ibid., 55–60.

20. Ibid., 60–62.

21. Summers and McDougald, *Programming on Radio and Television*, 9–12.

22. Sydney Head, *Broadcasting in America: A Survey of Television and Radio* (Boston: Houghton Mifflin, 1956), 137–38.

23. Summers and McDougald, *Programming on Radio and Television*, 12.

24. Head, *Broadcasting in America*, 139–40.

25. Summers and McDougald, *Programming on Radio and Television*, 13.

26. *Duncan v. U.S.*, 48 F2d 128 (1931); *KFKB Broadcasting Assn., Inc. v. FRC*, 47 F2d 670 (1931); and *Trinity Methodist Church, South, v. FRC*, 62 F2d 850 (1932). Also see Benjamin, *Freedom of the Air*, chapters 5–8.

27. Head, *Broadcasting in America*, 197–206 and 234–35.

28. Summers and McDougald, *Programming on Radio and Television*, 10–13.

2. An Advisory Council Is Formed

1. Robert K. Mueller, *The Director's and Officer's Guide to Advisory Boards* (New York: Quorum, 1990), 3–5.

2. Ibid., 5–6.

3. Minutes, RCA Board of Directors, January 6, 1922, ODY Papers, box 93, RCA Board of Directors; and E. P. Edwards to A. G. Davis, letter, January 6, 1922; Albert Davis to E. P. Edwards, letter, January 7, 1922; Albert G. Davis to E. W. Rice, letter, January 16, 1922; and Owen D. Young to E. M. Herr, E. W. Rice, and David Sarnoff (RCA Committee on Broadcasting), letter, July 19, 1922, ODY Papers, box 96, AT&T Wireless.

4. H. P. Davis, memorandum, October 12, 1925, Archive of Industrial Society, University of Pittsburgh, H. P. Davis Papers, box 3.

5. David Sarnoff, H. P. Davis, and Albert G. Davis, RCA Committee on Broadcasting, "To the Board of Directors, Radio Corporation of America," ODY Papers, box 93, RCA Board of Directors.

6. Minutes of the Board of Directors Meeting, January 22, 1926, ODY Papers, box 93, RCA Board of Directors.

7. David Sarnoff to J. G. Harbord, letter, July 15, 1926, ODY Papers, box 128, Broadcasting.

8. Report submitted by Ames and Norr, Inc., Public Relations Counsel, Radio Corporation of America, to Mr. Sarnoff, July 14, 1926, ODY Papers, box 128, Broadcasting.

9. Ibid.

10. Ibid.

11. Leslie H. Cochran, L. Allen Phelps, and Linda Letwin Cochran, *Advisory Committees in Action* (Boston: Allyn and Bacon, 1980), 6–7; Mueller, *Director's and Officer's Guide*, xi–xii and 1; Stephanie Smith, *Federal Advisory Committees: A Primer* (New York: Novinka, 2002), 2; Jacquelyn M. Cole and Maurice F. Cole, *Advisory Councils: A Theoretical and Practical Guide for Program Planners* (Englewood Cliffs, NJ: Prentice-Hall, 1983), 44–46; Richard A. Chapman, ed., *The Role of Commissions in Policy-Making* (London: George Allen and Unwin, 1973), 178–85; and Matthew V. Flinders and Martin J. Smith, eds., *Quangos, Accountability, and Reform: The Politics of Quasi-Government* (New York: St. Martin's Press, 1999), 37–43.

12. "WEAF Sold; Air Combine Is Forecast," New York *Tribune,* July 22, 1926, 1; and "WEAF Sale Only Part of Huge Deal," and "Coming Monopoly of Broadcasting by WEAF Is Seen," New York *World,* July 23, 1926, ODY Papers, box 128, Broadcasting.

13. "WEAF Sold," 1.

14. "WEAF Sale," and "Coming Monopoly."

15. Minutes of the Board of Directors of the Radio Corporation of America, August 10, 1926, ODY Papers, box 93, RCA Board of Directors.

16. Owen Young to M. H. Aylesworth, letter, November 16, 1926, ODY Papers, box 154, Advisory Council.

17. Chapman, *Role of Commissions*, 178–85, and Chris Skelcher, *The Appointed State: Quasi-governmental Organizations and Democracy* (Buckingham, UK: Open University Press, 1998), 60.

18. Mueller, *Director's and Officer's Guide*, 3–4, 43–48, and 119; and Cole and Cole, *Advisory Councils*, 44–46.

19. David Sarnoff, "Plan for the Support of National Broadcasting through Formation of the Public Broadcasting Company," August 12, 1925, AIS, H. P. Davis Papers, box 3.

20. Office of the President, RCA, to Board of Directors, RCA, letter, September 13, 1926, and minutes of the Board of Directors of the Radio Corporation of America, September 17, 1926, ODY Papers, box 93, RCA Board of Directors.

21. M. H. Aylesworth to Owen Young, letter, October 2, 1926, ODY Papers, box 154, Advisory Council; and "Opening Remarks Inaugural Program, National Broadcasting Company, Monday evening–November 15," delivered by Aylesworth, ODY Papers, box 128, Broadcasting.

22. Minutes of the Board of Directors of the Radio Corporation of America, September 17, 1926, ODY Papers, box 93, RCA Board of Directors.

23. The biographies noted here are drawn from the council members' *Who's Who* and *Who Was Who* biographies, as well as their obituaries, which appeared in various newspapers.

24. "Advisory Council National Broadcasting Company," memorandum, circa November 1, 1926; and Charles MacFarland to Stuart Parker, letter, April 25, 1927, ODY Papers, box 154, Advisory Council. Also see J. G. Harbord to Miss L. V. Morrison, letter, November 1, 1926, ODY Papers, box 154, Advisory Council.

25. Owen D. Young to Elihu Root, letter, November 6, 1926, ODY Papers, box 154, Advisory Council. The same or similar letters were sent to other proposed members.

26. Edwin Alderman to Owen Young, letter, November 12, 1926, ODY Papers, box 154, Advisory Council.

27. Morgan J. O'Brien to Owen Young, letter, November 10, 1926, ODY Papers, box 154, Advisory Council.

28. Owen Young to Charles E. Hughes, letter, November 18, 1926, ODY Papers, box 154, Advisory Council. Similar letters were sent to other invited members.

29. NBC Press Release, November 1, 1926, cited in Barnouw, *Tower in Babel*, 188; H. P. Davis to M. H. Aylesworth, letter, November 24, 1926, AIS, H. P. Davis Papers, box 3; and Merlin Aylesworth to Owen Young, letter, December 28, 1926, ODY Papers, box 128, Broadcasting.

30. Minutes of the Board of Directors of the National Broadcasting Company, Inc., December 3, 1926, ODY Papers, box 153, NBC–Board of Directors.

31. Mueller, *Director's and Officer's Guide*, 3–7.

32. "Memorandum of Minutes of the Advisory Council of the National

Broadcasting Company," first meeting, February 18, 1927, ODY Papers, box 154, Advisory Council.

33. Ibid.

34. Ibid.

35. See various letters in the Owen Young collection, including Young's letter to Charles E. Hughes, November 18, 1926, ODY Papers, box 154, Advisory Council.

36. Christopher Sterling and John Michael Kittross, *Stay Tuned: A History of American Broadcasting,* 3rd ed. (Mahwah, NJ: Erlbaum, 2002), 128.

37. Sterling and Kittross, *Stay Tuned,* 128–41 and 843–49.

3. Sustaining Program Development

1. Ellis Hawley, *The Great War and the Search for a Modern Order: A History of the American People and Their Institutions, 1917–1933* (New York: St. Martin's Press, 1979), 26–81; William Leuchtenburg, *The Perils of Prosperity, 1914–32* (Chicago: University of Chicago Press, 1967), 88–101; John D. Hicks, *The Republican Ascendency, 1921–1933* (New York: Harper and Row, 1960), 17–19; and Gerald Nash, *The Great Transition* (Boston: Allyn and Bacon, 1971), 171–73.

2. Donald McCoy, *Coming of Age* (Middlesex, UK: Penguin Books, 1973), 76–81 and 109; Hawley, *Great War and the Search for a Modern Order,* 61–69 and 104–5; Leuchtenburg, *Perils of Prosperity,* 101–3; Hicks, *Republican Ascendency,* 195–98; and Nash, *Great Transition,* 172–73.

3. "Memorandum of Minutes of the Advisory Council of the National Broadcasting Company," second meeting, March 7, 1928, and first draft of letter "To the Members of the Advisory Council of the National Broadcasting Company," n.d., ODY Papers, box 154, Advisory Council.

4. Memorandum of minutes of second meeting; "Advisory Council of the National Broadcasting Company: Committee Reports, the President's Report" (second meeting), ODY Papers, box 154, Advisory Council

5. Ibid.

6. Handwritten notes of the second meeting of the Advisory Council of the National Broadcasting Company, and memorandum of minutes of second meeting; ODY Papers, box 154, Advisory Council.

7. Memorandum of minutes of second meeting; "Advisory Council of the National Broadcasting Company: Committee Reports, the President's Report" (second meeting), ODY Papers, box 154, Advisory Council.

8. Memorandum of minutes of second meeting, ODY Papers, box 154, Advisory Council.

9. Mullen to Farrell, letter, June 5, 1929; memorandum for Prof. C. F. Marvin, May 29, 1929; Farrell to Mullen, letter, August 14, 1928; Aylesworth to Farrell, letter, August 21, 1928; Mullen to Farrell, letter, September 18, 1929; and Morse Salisbury to T. B. Symons, letter, June 1, 1929, Kansas State Libraries, Morse Special Collections.

10. Frank Mullen to F. D. Farrell, telegram, June 17, 1929, and "NBC Press Release: for Release July 9 or later," Kansas State Libraries, Morse Special Collections.

11. "Advisory Council of the National Broadcasting Company, Third Meeting, 1929," ODY Papers, box 159, Advisory Council.

12. Ibid., and Press Relations Department, "Special Release," n.d., ODY Papers, box 154, Advisory Council.

13. F. D. Farrell to F. E. Mullen, letter, June 18, 1929, Kansas State Libraries, Morse Special Collections.

14. Frank Mullen to F. D. Farrell, letter, July 10, 1929, Kansas State Libraries, Morse Special Collections.

15. "Press Release: For Release Afternoon Papers September 28," Kansas State Libraries, Morse Special Collections.

16. Frank Mullen to Francis D. Farrell, Pres., Kansas State College, letter, January 11, 1930, Kansas State Libraries, Morse Special Collections.

17. Ibid.

18. "Advisory Council of the National Broadcasting Company: The President's Report and Resume of Programs, Committee Reports," fourth meeting, 1930, ODY Papers, file 11-14-82, box 156, Advisory Council.

19. Memorandum of minutes of the fifth meeting of the Advisory Council of the National Broadcasting Company, ODY Papers, file 11-14-82, box 157, Advisory Council.

20. "Advisory Council of the National Broadcasting Company: The President's Report and Resume of Programs, Committee Reports, Fifth Meeting, 1931," ODY Papers, file 11-14-82, box 159, Advisory Council.

21. Memorandum of minutes of fifth meeting, ODY Papers, file 11-14-82, box 157, Advisory Council.

22. Ibid.

23. Ibid.

24. Frank Mullen to Francis Farrell, letter, January 1, 1931, and Frank Mullen to Francis Farrell, letter, January 11, 1931, Kansas State Libraries, Morse Special Collections; and "Advisory Council of the National Broadcasting Company: The President's Report and Resume of Programs, Committee Reports, Fifth Meeting, 1931," ODY Papers, file 11-14-82, box 159, Advisory Council.

25. Ibid.

26. Interoffice memo, "Report on Activities of the Agricultural Department for the Month of June," June 24, 1931, Kansas State Libraries, Morse Special Collections.

27. F. D. Farrell to Frank Mullen, letter, September 12, 1931; interoffice memo, "Report on Activities of the Agricultural Department for the Month of June," June 24, 1931; and interoffice memo, "Activities in the Agricultural Department during July," July 24, 1931, Kansas State Libraries, Morse Special Collections.

28. Mullen to Farrell, letter, January 12, 1933, with "Report of Agriculture Department for 1932," Kansas State Libraries, Morse Special Collections.

29. "Activities in the Agricultural Department," October 1, 1931, and Frank Mullen to Francis Farrell, letter, September 17, 1931, with press release, Kansas State Libraries, Morse Special Collections.

30. "Activities in the Agricultural Department during December," January 4, 1932, Kansas State Libraries, Morse Special Collections.

31. "Activities in the Agricultural Department during June," July 1, 1932, Kansas State Libraries, Morse Special Collections.

32. "Monthly Report July," August 1, 1932; Mullen to Farrell, letter, October 12, 1932, with "The NBC Agricultural Policy"; and Mullen to Farrell, letter, January 12, 1933, with "Report of Agriculture Department for 1932," Kansas State Libraries, Morse Special Collections.

33. Mullen to Farrell, letter, January 12, 1933, with "Report of Agriculture Department for 1932," Kansas State Libraries, Morse Special Collections.

34. Ibid.

35. "Advisory Council of the National Broadcasting Company: President's Report and Resume of Programs, Committee Reports," fifth meeting, 1931, ODY Papers, file 11-14-82, box 159, Advisory Council.

36. Christopher Sterling and John Michael Kittross, *Stay Tuned: A History of American Broadcasting, Third Edition* (Mahwah, NJ: Erlbaum, 2002), 826 and 862.

37. "Advisory Council of the National Broadcasting Company: President's Report and Resume of Programs, Committee Reports," seventh meeting, 1933, ODY Papers, file 11-14-82, box 161, Advisory Council.

38. Ibid.

39. F. D. Farrell to F. E. Mullen, letter, April 6, 1933, and Mullen to Farrell, letter, April 4, 1933, with "Report on Agricultural Activities for March 1933," Kansas State Libraries, Morse Special Collections.

40. Frank Mullen to Milton Eisenhower, letter, March 29, 1933, and Eisenhower to Mullen, letter, April 6, 1933, Kansas State Libraries, Morse Special Collections.

41. Frank Mullen to Milton Eisenhower, letter, March 29, 1933; Eisenhower to Mullen, letter, April 6, 1933; and Frank "Scoop" Russell to Frank Mullen, memo, April 4, 1933, Kansas State Libraries, Morse Special Collections.

42. "Advisory Council of the National Broadcasting Company: President's Report and Resume of Programs, Committee Reports," seventh meeting, 1933, ODY Papers, file 11-14-82, box 161, Advisory Council.

43. "Advisory Council of the National Broadcasting Company: President's Report and Resume of Programs, Committee Reports," eighth meeting, 1934, ODY Papers, file 11-14-82, box 161, Advisory Council.

44. Ibid.

45. Milton Eisenhower to Frank Mullen, letter, December 29, 1933, Kansas State Libraries, Morse Special Collections, cited in "Advisory Council of the National Broadcasting Company: President's Report and Resume of Programs,

Committee Reports," eighth meeting, 1934, ODY Papers, file 11-14-82, box 161, Advisory Council.

46. "Advisory Council of the National Broadcasting Company: President's Report and Resume of Programs, Committee Reports," eighth meeting, 1934, ODY papers, file 11-14-82, box 161, Advisory Council.

47. Ibid.

48. "Report of the Chairman, Committee on Agriculture," n.d., Kansas State Libraries, Morse Special Collections.

49. F. D. Farrell to William E. Drips, letter, April 27, 1937; Drips to Farrell, letter, April 12, 1937; William Drips to Morse Salisbury, letter, April 12, 1937; and William Drips to Francis D. Farrell, letter, January 6, 1937, with "Annual Report of the National Farm and Home Hour, 1936," Kansas State Libraries, Morse Special Collections.

50. William Drips to Francis Farrell, letter, March 26, 1938; and script, *National Farm and Home Hour*, June 7, 1938, Kansas State Libraries, Morse Special Collections.

51. Script, *National Farm and Home Hour*, June 7, 1938, Kansas State Libraries, Morse Special Collections.

52. Memorandum for the Secretary, July 5, 1938, Kansas State Libraries, Morse Special Collections.

53. Press release, "Regional Farm Programs to Augment Farm and Home Hour," August 15, 1938; Lohr to Secretary of Agriculture, letter, August 17, 1938; and W. E. Drips to Francis Farrell, letter, September 6, 1938, Kansas State Libraries, Morse Special Collections.

54. Farrell to Lohr, letter, September 9, 1938, Kansas State Libraries, Morse Special Collections.

55. Angell to Farrell, letter, September 14, 1938, Kansas State Libraries, Morse Special Collections.

56. Lohr to Farrell, letter, September 21, 1938, Kansas State Libraries, Morse Special Collections.

57. Drips to Farrell, letter, February 29, 1940; Farrell to Drips, letter, July 5, 1939; and Drips to Farrell, letter, June 30, 1939, with "Monthly Report, Agricultural Department, June, 1939," Kansas State Libraries, Morse Special Collections.

58. Drips to Farrell, letter, December 16, 1941, with "Monthly Report, Agricultural Department, November, 1941," Kansas State Libraries, Morse Special Collections.

59. Drips to Farrell, letter, January 5, 1942, Kansas State Libraries, Morse Special Collections.

60. Teacher's guide, NBC *Music Appreciation Hour*, 1939–40, Library of Congress, NBC Papers, file 211.

61. "Detailed Report on Music Appreciation Hour," January 10, 1930, Library of Congress, NBC Papers, file 209.

62. Ibid.

63. Ibid.

64. "Report on the Music Appreciation Hour, 1930, to Mr. Elwood," Library of Congress, NBC Papers, File 209.

65. Ibid.

66. NBC *Music Appreciation Hour*, teacher's guide, 1939–40, Library of Congress, NBC Papers, file 211.

67. "The NBC *Music Appreciation Hour*, Walter Damrosch, Conductor," 1933, Library of Congress, NBC Papers, file 208, and NBC *Music Appreciation Hour*, student notebooks, 1932–33 and 1939–40, Library of Congress, NBC Papers, files 210 and 211.

68. Letter to Richard C. Patterson, October 22, 1935, Library of Congress, NBC Papers, file 208.

69. Announcement, *Music Appreciation Hour*, sixth season, 1933–34, Library of Congress, NBC Papers, file 210; Library of Congress, NBC Papers, file 208.

70. "Advisory Council of the National Broadcasting Company: The President's Report and Resume of Programs, Committee Reports, Fifth Meeting, 1931," ODY Papers, file 11-14-82, box 159, Advisory Council.

71. Memorandum of minutes of the fifth meeting of the Advisory Council of the National Broadcasting Company, ODY Papers, file 11-14-82, box 157, Advisory Council.

72. Ibid.

73. Memorandum of minutes of the sixth meeting of the Advisory Council of the National Broadcasting Company, February 16, 1932, ODY Papers, file 11-14-82, box 158, Advisory Council.

74. Ibid.

75. Ibid.

76. Ibid.

77. ENC to Young, internal correspondence, January 21, 1932, and February 1, 1932; memorandum to Young regarding items on the agenda of the Advisory Council meeting, February 15, 1932; ENC to Morgan J. O'Brien, letter, February 26, 1932; ENC to Walter Lippman, letter, April 21, 1932; ODY to Walter Lippman, letter, April 21, 1932; Walter Lippman to Everett Case, letter, April 25, 1932; and ENC to Walter Lippman, letter, May 4, 1932, ODY Papers, file 11-14-82, box 158, Advisory Council.

78. "Advisory Council of the National Broadcasting Company: The President's Report and Resume of Programs, Committee Reports, Seventh Meeting, February, 1933," ODY Papers, file 11-14-82, box 161, Advisory Council.

79. Ibid.

80. Ibid.

81. Ibid.

82. Ibid.

83. Memorandum of minutes of the eighth meeting of the Advisory Council of the National Broadcasting Company, and "Advisory Council of the National

Broadcasting Company, the President's Report and Resume of Programs, Committee Reports, Eighth Meeting, April 18, 1934," ODY Papers, file 11-14-82, box 161, Advisory Council.

4. Religious Issues and the Advisory Council

1. Ellis Hawley, *The Great War and the Search for a Modern Order: A History of the American People and Their Institutions, 1917–1933* (New York: St. Martin's Press, 1979), 137; and William Leuchtenburg, *The Perils of Prosperity, 1914–32* (Chicago: University of Chicago Press, 1967), 158, 170–71.

2. Hawley, *Great War*, 146–48.

3. Hawley, *Great War*, 86, 137–39, 168–69; and Leuchtenburg, *Perils of Prosperity*, 158, 168–71.

4. Hawley, *Great War*, 72–73, 107–8, and Leuchtenburg, *Perils of Prosperity*, 207–9.

5. Sterling and Kittross, *Stay Tuned*, 128.

6. Memorandum to the National Broadcasting Company from the Committee of Religious Activities of the Advisory Council, n.d., circa December 1927; memorandum of minutes of the second meeting of the Advisory Council of the National Broadcasting Company, March 7, 1928; "Advisory Council of the National Broadcasting Company: Committee Reports, the President's Report"; Charles MacFarland to Stuart Parker, letter, April 25, 1927; Merlin Aylesworth to Charles MacFarland, letter, November 15, 1927; Charles MacFarland to Merlin Aylesworth, letter, November 18, 1927; Charles MacFarland to Owen Young, letter, January 11, 1928; ODY Papers, box 154, Advisory Council.

7. Memorandum of minutes of second meeting, ODY Papers, box 154, Advisory Council.

8. "Advisory Council of the National Broadcasting Company, Third Meeting, 1929," ODY Papers, box 159, Advisory Council.

9. Ibid.

10. A. R. Goux to E. N. Case, letter, January 28, 1929, and A. R. Goux to Advisory Council, letter, January 29, 1929; memorandum of minutes of the third meeting of the Advisory Council of the National Broadcasting Company, January 30, 1929, ODY Papers, box 156, Advisory Council.

11. Memorandum of minutes of the third meeting of the Advisory Council of the National Broadcasting Company, January 30, 1929, ODY Papers, box 156, Advisory Council.

12. A. R. Goux to Everett Case, letter, January 30, 1929, ODY Papers, box 156, Advisory Council.

13. Aylesworth to A. R. Goux, letter, May 5, 1928, ODY Papers, file 11-14-82, box 157, Advisory Council.

14. Merlin Aylesworth to Everett Case, letter, February 6, 1929, ODY Papers, box 156, Advisory Council.

15. Memorandum of minutes of the third meeting of the Advisory Council

of the National Broadcasting Company, January 30, 1929, ODY Papers, box 156, Advisory Council; and Everett Case to A. R. Goux, letter, January 31, 1929, ODY Papers, box 156, Advisory Council.

16. Watch Tower Bible and Tract Society to Owen Young, letter, September 3, 1931; Watch Tower Bible and Tract Society to Station Manager, letter, September 3, 1931; and Watch Tower B & T Society to Owen Young, letter, October 6, 1931, ODY Papers, file 11-14-82, box 157, Advisory Council.

17. Watch Tower Society to Owen Young, letter, September 15, 1931, ODY Papers, file 11-14-82, box 157, Advisory Council.

18. Watch Tower Society to Owen Young, letter, November 9, 1931, ODY Papers, file 11-14-82, box 158, Advisory Council; and Watch Tower Society to Francis D. Farrell, letter, November 18, 1931, Kansas State University, Morse Department of Special Collections.

19. Agenda, Advisory Council of the National Broadcasting Company, sixth meeting, February 16, 1932, ODY Papers, file 11-14-82, box 157, Advisory Council.

20. E. N. Case to Young, memorandum, February 15, 1932, ODY Papers, file 11-14-82, box 157, Advisory Council.

21. Handwritten notes on meeting, and memorandum of minutes of the sixth meeting of the Advisory Council of the National Broadcasting Company, February 16, 1932, ODY Papers, file 11-14-82, box 157, Advisory Council.

22. Memorandum of minutes of the sixth meeting of the Advisory Council of the National Broadcasting Company, February 16, 1932, ODY Papers, file 11-14-82, box 157, Advisory Council.

23. ENC (Everett Case) to Watch Tower Bible and Tract Society, letter, February 29, 1932, ODY Papers, file 11-14-82, box 157, Advisory Council.

24. Memorandum of minutes of the sixth meeting of the Advisory Council of the National Broadcasting Company, February 16, 1932, ODY Papers, file 11-14-82, box 158, Advisory Council.

25. John Cahalan Jr., "The Hour of Power," *Commonweal*, January 28, 1931, 343–45.

26. Ibid.

27. Alan Brinkley, *Voices of Dissent: Huey Long, Father Coughlin, and the Great Depression* (New York: Knopf, 1982).

28. Lauter and Friend, "Radio and the Censors," 359–65. Also cited in Hutchinson, "Is the Air Already Monopolized?"

29. Jane Butler, CBS, "The Case of Father Coughlin," letter to the editor, *Christian Century*, March 23, 1932.

30. "The Coughlin Puzzle," *Michigan Christian Advocate*, December 24, 1931, 5, National Archives, RG-173, FCC General Correspondence, 1927–71, box 199, file 44-3: Rev. Charles E. Coughlin.

31. Minutes of board of directors meeting, January 5, 1931, ACLU Papers, Seely Mudd Library, Princeton University.

32. Memorandum to Colonel Brown, February 8, 1933, RG-173, FCC General Correspondence, 1927–71, box 199, file 44–3: Rev. Charles E. Coughlin.

33. "Deplores 'Too Much Talk,'" *New York Times*, April 18, 1932, 17.

34. "Priest Defends His Radio Talks," New York Times, May 10, 1932, 23.

35. Leo Fitzpatrick to Malcolm Bingay, letter, March 30, 1933, RG-173, FCC General Correspondence, 1927–71, box 199, file 44–3: Rev. Charles E. Coughlin.

36. C. B. Jolliffe, chief engineer, to Commission, memorandum, December 7, 1933, RG-173, FCC General Correspondence, 1927–71, box 199, file 44–3: Rev. Charles E. Coughlin.

37. "Coughlin condemns Our Policy in Mexico," New York *Times*, December 24, 1934, 9.

38. Correspondence, November 1938, RG-173, FCC General Correspondence, 1927–71, box 200, file 44–3: Rev. Charles E. Coughlin.

39. "Advisory Council of the National Broadcasting Company: The President's Report and Resume of Programs, Committee Reports," seventh meeting, February 1933, ODY Papers, file 11-14-82, box 161, Advisory Council.

40. Ibid.

41. Memorandum of minutes of the ninth meeting of the Advisory Council of the National Broadcasting Company, May 27, 1935, ODY Papers, file 11-14-82, box 162, Advisory Council.

42. Memorandum of minutes of the eighth meeting of the Advisory Council of the National Broadcasting Company, April 18, 1934, ODY Papers, file 11-14-82, box 161, Advisory Council.

43. Brinkley, *Voices of Dissent.*

44. Young to Mrs. August Belmont, letter, December 15, 1938, ODY Papers, file 11-14-82, box 162, Advisory Council.

45. Young to Al Smith, letter, December 30, 1938, ODY Papers, file 11-14-82, box 162, Advisory Council.

46. Smith to Young, letter, January 4, 1939, ODY Papers, file 11-14-82, box 162, Advisory Council.

47. Sarnoff to Young, letter, February 6, 1939, ODY Papers, file 11-14-82, box 162, Advisory Council.

48. Memorandum of minutes of the twelfth meeting of the Advisory Council of the National Broadcasting Company, January 9, 1939, ODY Papers, file 11-14-82, box 162, Advisory Council.

49. Ibid.

50. Ibid.

51. Ibid.

52. Ibid.

53. Ibid.

54. Ibid

55. Ibid.

56. Ibid.

57. Ibid.

58. Memorandum for Mr. Sarnoff regarding the Advisory Council, February 2, 1939, and Sarnoff to Young, letter, February 6, 1939, ODY Papers, file 11-14-82, box 162, Advisory Council; and *Brief History of the Advisory Council of the National Broadcasting Company with Digest of Its Important Actions . . . March 1, 1939*, Wisconsin State Historical Society, NBC Papers, Advisory Council, Reports and Minutes, 1927–36, box 107, file: History 1939.

5. The Council and Radio Coverage of Birth Control

1. C. R. McCann, *Birth Control Politics in the United States, 1916–1945* (Ithaca, NY: Cornell University Press, 1994), 15–17.

2. Ibid., 26–27.

3. Ibid., 1–15.

4. L. Gordon, *The Moral Property of Women: A History of Birth Control Politics in America,* 3d ed. (Urbana: University of Illinois Press, 2002), 201.

5. McCann, *Birth Control Politics*, 134.

6. Gordon, *Moral Property of Women*, 242.

7. McCann, *Birth Control Politics*, 57.

8. "Dr. Parran Quits Council," New York *Times*, November 21, 1934, 20.

9. F. Bailey to Mrs. F. Robertson Jones, letter, October 24, 1930; Gustav Peck, speech, "Economic Philosophies," Fourth Talk: Thomas Robert Malthus, October 8, 1930, 3:45, and G. Peck to Harry Elmer Barnes, letter, October 17, 1930, Seely Mudd Library, ACLU Papers, vol. 431; and V. Lauter and J. Friend, "Radio and the Censors," *Forum*, December 1931, 359–65.

10. J. Rorty, "The Impending Radio War," *Harper's Monthly Magazine*, vol. 163, November 1931, 725.

11. Committee of Religious Activities of the Advisory Council to the National Broadcasting Company, memorandum, n.d., circa December 1927, and minutes of the second meeting of the Advisory Council of the National Broadcasting Company, March 7, 1928, ODY Papers, box 154, Advisory Council.

12. "Air Censorship on Birth Control Talks Assailed," New York *Herald Tribune*, January 17, 1930, and "Birth Control Group Criticizes Radio Ban," Buffalo *Evening News*, January 17, 1930, ACLU Papers, vol. 385.

13. ACLU to John Elwood, letter, November 22, 1929, ACLU Papers, vol. 375.

14. ACLU to Elwood, letter, November 22, 1929, and H. W. Ward, letters to Walter Damrosch and Ira E. Robinson, November 23, 1929, ACLU Papers, vol. 375.

15. C. Butman to Harry Ward, letter, December 17, 1929; F. D. Farrell to Harry F. Ward, letter, November 26, 1929; F. H. Lovette to Harry F. Ward, letter, November 26, 1929; C. MacFarland to Harry Ward, letter, November 27, 1929; and I. Robinson to Harry F. Ward, letter, November 29, 1929, ACLU Papers, vol. 375.

16. O. D. Young to Harry Ward, letter, December 3, 1929, ACLU Papers, vol. 375.

17. Ibid.

18. Ibid.

19. H. W. Ward to Owen Young, letter, December 10, 1929, ACLU Papers, vol. 375.

20. Ibid.

21. Ibid.

22. "Advisory Council of the National Broadcasting Company: The President's Report and Resume of Programs, Committee Reports," fourth meeting, 1930, ODY Papers, file 11-14-82, box 156, Advisory Council.

23. "Detailed Report," February 14, 1930, ODY Papers, file 11-14-82, box 156, Advisory Council.

24. Ibid.

25. Ibid.

26. Ibid.

27. Ibid.

28. Ibid.

29. Ibid.

30. F. Bailey to Everett Case, letter, February 14, 1930; E. Case to Harry Ward, letter, February 13, 1930; and Case, E. (1930b), to Forrest Bailey, letter, February 20, 1930, ACLU Papers, vol. 431.

31. "Protests Radio Chain Ban," New York *Times*, November 26, 1929, and "Leaders Point the Way to New Opportunities," New York *Times*, February 12, 1930, 12.

32. ACLU press release, "For Release Tuesday," March 25, 1930, ACLU Papers, vol. 431, and "Birth Control Group Criticizes Radio Ban," Buffalo *Evening News*, January 17, 1930, ACLU Papers, vol. 385.

33. M. Toffefson to Forrest Bailey, letter, January 13, 1930, and F. Bailey to Maude Toffefson, letter, January 14, 1930, ACLU Papers, vol. 385.

34. "Detailed Report," February 14, ODY Papers, file 11-14-82, box 156, Advisory Council.

35. Mary Sherman to Everett Case, letter, February 27, 1933, ODY Papers, box 156, Advisory Council.

6. The Council and Controversial Political Broadcasts

1. "Minutes of the First Annual Convention of the National Association of Broadcasters," Broadcast Pioneers Collection, Library of American Broadcasting, file VF-NAB-History.

2. "Minutes of the Third Annual Meeting of the National Association of Broadcasters on September 16–17, 1925," NAB files.

3. William G. Shepard, "Blotting Out the Blah," *Colliers*, August 23, 1924, 11.

4. "Coolidge Rebuff in Dill Radio Bill," New York *World*, May 7, 1926, ACLU Papers, 1926, vol. 300.

5. Isabelle Kendig to Lucille Milner, letter, May 5, 1926, ACLU Papers, 1926, vol. 310.

6. Memorandum of minutes of the second meeting of the Advisory Council of the National Broadcasting Company, March 7, 1928; "Advisory Council of the National Broadcasting Company: Committee Reports, the President's Report," ODY Papers, box 154, Advisory Council.

7. Ibid.

8. Handwritten notes of the second meeting and typed memorandum of minutes of the second meeting, ODY, box 154, Advisory Council.

9. "Large Radio Chain in June for National Conclaves," New York *Times*, February 12, 1928, sec. 9, 14.

10. "Campaign Expected to Aid Broadcasters," New York *Times*, March 11, 1928, sec. 9, 15.

11. Owen Comora, "From McNamee to Huntley -Brinkley: 40 Years of Political Convention Broadcasting," *Electronic Age*, 23, no. 3 (summer 1964), and Quin Ryan, "Quin Ryan Recalls Early Conventions," Chicago *Tribune*, Sunday, July 12, 1964, Radio section, 10, in BPL, 82: Broadcasting in Political Campaigns.

12. Newspaper clipping, "Voice Personality Will Count in Race to the White House," Wisconsin State Historical Society Archives, Martin Codel Papers, box 6, file: Misc. Loose Papers.

13. Newspaper clipping, "Brevity and Appeal to Reason Make Radio Talks Magnetic," MCHC, Martin Codel Papers, box 6, file: Misc. Loose Papers.

14. Graham McNamee, "The Elephant and the Donkey Take the Air," *American Magazine*, November 1928, 15.

15. Ibid., 153.

16. Frank R. Kent, "The Great Game of Politics," MCHC, Martin Codel Papers, box 6, file: Misc. Loose Papers.

17. Henry Pritchett to M. H. Aylesworth, letter, October 23, 1928; M. H. Aylesworth to Henry Pritchett, letter, October 26, 1928; F. D. Farrell to M. H. Aylesworth, letter, November 5, 1928, ODY Papers, box 154, Advisory Council.

18. Owen Young to the Members of the Advisory Council, January 30, 1929, ODY Papers, box 156, Advisory Council.

19. Ibid., and Advisory Council of the National Broadcasting Company, Third Meeting, 1929, ODY Papers, box 159, Advisory Council.

20. Memorandum of minutes of the third meeting of the Advisory Council of the National Broadcasting Company, January 30, 1929, ODY Papers, box 156, Advisory Council.

21. Advisory Council of the National Broadcasting Company, Third Meeting, 1929, ODY Papers, box 159, Advisory Council.

22. Ellis Hawley, *The Great War and the Search for a Modern Order: A History of the American People and Their Institutions, 1917–1933* (New York: St. Martin's Press, 1979), 173–91.

23. Ibid., 173–84.

24. Ibid., 180–85.

25. Sterling and Kittross, *Stayed Tuned*, 141–96.

26. Benjamin, *Freedom of the Air*, 114–17.

27. Ibid., 117–22.

28. Ibid., 122–27.

29. Ibid., 127.

30. "Radio Prepares for Barrage of Political Oratory," New York *Times*, June 5, 1932, sec. 10, 8.

31. Orrin E. Dunlap Jr., "Two Hundred Broadcasters Join Convention Hook-Up," New York *Times*, June 12, 1932, sec. 9, 5.

32. "Mail Reveals American's Reaction to Politics on the Air," New York *Times*, July 17, 1932, section 8, 5.

33. Orrin E. Dunlap, Jr., "Lessons of the Campaign," New York *Times*, November 13, 1932, section 8, 6; and "Radio Broadcasting in the 1932 Campaign," Wisconsin State Historical Society Archives, Mass Communication Ephemera Collection, box 5: National Association of Broadcasters—General.

34. "Radio 'Debunking' the Campaigns," *Literary Digest*, December 1, 1928.

35. Hawley, *Great War*, 213–29.

36. "Preparing for the Crusade," New York *Times*, September 4, 1932.

37. "Personal Touch Survives," New York *Times*, October 29, 1932, 14.

38. Orrin E. Dunlap Jr., "Lessons of the Campaign," New York *Times*, November 13, 1932, sec. 8, 6.

39. "Politics Irks Broadcasters," New York *Times*, October 23, 1932, sec. 8, 6, and "Politics on Air Ousts Regular Programs," New York *Times*, November 2, 1934, 16.

40. "Campaign Wind-Up Upsets Radio Plans," New York *Times*, November 4, 1932, 11.

41. "Broadcasters Plan Busy Days," New York *Times*, October 30, 1932, sec. 8, 6.

42. Orrin E. Dunlap Jr., "Elaborate Plans for Tuesday," New York *Times*, November 6, 1932, sec. 8, 6.

43. Hawley, *Great War*, 213–29.

44. "Radio and the New Oratory," editorial, *Christian Century*, November 30, 1932, 146.

45. "Today's Town Crier," editorial, New York *Times*, November 6, 1930, 24.

46. "Advisory Council of the National Broadcasting Company: The President's Report and Resume of Programs, Committee Reports, Seventh Meeting, February, 1933," ODY Papers, file 11-14-82, box 161, Advisory Council.

47. Ibid.

48. "President Employs Air, Press to Educate Nation," *Literary Digest*, January 27, 1934, 9.

49. "Roosevelt and Cabinet," New York *Times*, December 24, 1934, 9.

50. "Roosevelt Bars Radio in Talk to Bankers; To Keep Broadcasts for 'Fireside Chats,'" New York *Times*, October 9, 1934, 2.

51. "Party Control for Official Radio Talks," New York *Times*, September 24, 1933, reprinted in ANPA Bulletin, no. 6179, October 6, 1933.

52. Memorandum of minutes of the eighth meeting of the Advisory Council of the National Broadcasting Company, April 18, 1934, ODY Papers, file 11-14-82, box 161, Advisory Council.

53. Ibid.

54. Ibid.

55. ENC to Young, memo, May 27, 1935, ODY Papers, file 11-14-82, box 162, Advisory Council.

56. Memorandum of minutes of the ninth meeting of the Advisory Council of the National Broadcasting Company, May 27, 1935, and Hitchins to Young, letter, May 17, 1935, ODY Papers, file 11-14-82, box 162, Advisory Council.

57. Ibid.

58. Ibid.

59. Ibid.

60. Memorandum of minutes of the tenth meeting of the Advisory Council of the National Broadcasting Company, May 7, 1936, ODY Papers, file 11-14-82, box 162, Advisory Council.

61. Ibid.

62. "$1,000,000 on Air for G.O.P.," New York *Times*, January 13, 1936, 2.

63. *Liberty at the Cross Roads*, January 8, 1936, RWC 6208, B2–3, NBC Collection, Library of Congress.

64. Ibid.

65. Lenox Lohr to Henry Fletcher, letter, January 8, 1936, Library of Congress, NBC Papers, folder 371.

66. "Political Broadcasts, a Series of Letters Exchanged between the Columbia Broadcast System, Inc., and the Republican National Committee," NBC Papers, folder 371.

67. Ibid.

68. Ibid.

69. "Party Head Reveals Ban," New York *Times*, January 14, 1936, 17.

70. "Appeal by Air," editorial, Washington *Post*, January 15, 1936.

71. Memorandum of minutes of the tenth meeting of the Advisory Council of the National Broadcasting Company, May 7, 1936, ODY Papers, file 11-14-82, box 162, Advisory Council.

72. Ibid., and "Political Broadcasts," ODY Papers, file 11-14- 82, box 162, Advisory Council.

73. "Purchase of Time by Communist Party," and minutes of the tenth meeting, May 7, 1936, ODY Papers, file 11-14-82, box 162, Advisory Council.

74. Paul Butler Jr., *Presidential Campaigns* (New York: Oxford University Press, 1985), 242.

75. "G.O.P. Dramatizes What It Terms Dictatorship and Abuse of Relief," *Christian Science Monitor*, January 22, 1936, 8

76. Ibid.

77. "New Deal Assailed," Washington *Post*, February 5, 1936, 7.

78. "Radio to Elect Next President," *Christian Science Monitor*, February 26, 1936.

79. "Losers in Election Used Radio More," New York *Times*, December 10, 1936, 12; "The Final 'Words,'" New York *Times*, October 25, 1936, X12; and Orrin Dunlap, "A Voice of Victory," New York *Times*, November 8, 1936, X12.

80. Orrin Dunlap, "Act II Begins," New York *Times*, January 17, 1937, 164, and "World Will Hear Inaugural Events," New York *Times*, January 20, 1937, 9.

7. Controversial Issues of Public Importance

1. Sterling and Kitross, *Stay Tuned* , 180–207 and 843–49.

2. H. H. Heath to Basil Mitchell, letter, June 24, 1948, ODY Papers, file 11-14-82, box 164, Advisory Council.

3. Memorandum of minutes of the eleventh meeting of the Advisory Council of the National Broadcasting Company, April 12, 1938, ODY Papers, file 11-14-82, box 162, Advisory Council.

4. Ibid.

5. Ibid.

6. Ibid.

7. Ibid.

8. Ibid.

9. Ibid.

10. Ibid.

11. Ibid.

12. Ibid.

13. Sarnoff to Young, letter, February 6, 1939, ODY Papers, file 11-14-82, box 162, Advisory Council.

14. Memorandum of minutes of the twelfth meeting of the Advisory Council of the National Broadcasting Company, January 9, 1939, ODY Papers, file 11-14-82, box 162, Advisory Council.

15. Ibid.

16. Ibid.

17. David Sarnoff, "Principles and Practices of Network Radio Broadcasting," hearings before the Federal Communications Commission, November 14, 1938.

18. Memorandum of minutes of the twelfth meeting, January 9, 1939, ODY Papers, file 11-14-82, box 162, Advisory Council.

19. Memorandum for Mr. Sarnoff regarding the Advisory Council, February 2, 1939, ODY Papers, file 11-14-82, box 162, Advisory Council.

20. Ibid.

21. Ibid.

22. Ibid.

23. Sarnoff to Young, letter, February 6, 1939, ODY papers, file 11-14-82, box 162, Advisory Council.

24. *Brief History of the Advisory Council of the National Broadcasting Company with Digest of its Important Actions . . . March 1, 1939,* Wisconsin State Historical Society, NBC Papers, Advisory Council, Reports and Minutes, 1927–1936, box 107, file: History 1939.

25. FCC, *Mayflower Decision*, 8 FCC 333.

26. "Broadcasting in Time of War," Library of Congress, NBC Papers, file 642, World War II.

27. Ibid.

28. Ibid.

29. Ibid.

30. Ibid.

31. Ibid.

32. Ibid.

33. Ibid.

34. C. A. Spoul to Owen Young, letter, June 10, 1940, ODY Papers, file 11-14-82, box 164, Advisory Council.

35. Owen Young to C. A. Spoul, letter, July 3, 1940, ODY Papers, file 11-14-82, box 164, Advisory Council.

36. Phillips Carlin to Lillian Morrison, letter, June 13, 1940, ODY Papers, file 11-14-82, box 164, Advisory Council.

37. James Angell to Owen Young, letter, January 31, 1941, ODY Papers, file 11-14-82, box 164, Advisory Council.

38. Agenda for meeting of the Advisory Council of the National Broadcasting Company, February 28, 1941, and minutes of the thirteenth meeting of the Advisory Council of the National Broadcasting Company, February 28, 1941, ODY Papers, file 11-14-82, box 164, Advisory Council.

39. Ibid.

40. Ibid.

41. James Angell to Owen Young, letter, April 21, 1941, ODY Papers, file 11-14-82, box 164, Advisory Council.

42. Owen Young to John Davis, letter, February 6, 1945, ODY Papers, file 11-14-82, box 164, Advisory Council.

43. Owen Young to Niles Trammell, letter, January 23, 1945; Niles Trammell to Owen Young, letters, January 15, 1945, and February 5, 1945; Owen Young

to John Davis, letter, February 6, 1945; J. G. Harbord to Owen Young, letter, February 16, 1945; and L. MacConnach to Owen Young, letter, April 11, 1945, ODY Papers, file 11-14-82, box 164, Advisory Council.

44. L. MacConnach to Owen Young, letter, April 11, 1945, ODY Papers, file 11-14-82, box 164, Advisory Council.

45. Owen Young to Niles (Trammell), letter, January 23, 1945, ODY Papers, file 11-14-82, box 164, Advisory Council.

46. Niles Trammell to Owen Young, letter, January 15, 1945, ODY Paper, file 11-14-82, box 164, Advisory Council.

47. Josephine Young Case and Everett Needham Case, *Owen D. Young and American Enterprise* (Boston: Godine, 1982), 765.

48. J. G. Harbord to Owen Young, letter, February 16, 1945, ODY Papers, file 11-14-82, box 164, Advisory Council.

8. Epilogue

1. FCC, *Report on Chain Broadcasting* (Washington, DC: Government Printing Office, 1941), 31.

2. U.S. Census, Bureau of Economic Analysis, Table 657, Selected Per Capita Income and Product Items in Current and Real (2000) Dollars: 1929 to 2006, Statistical Abstract of the United States, Washington, DC: Government Printing Office, 2006.

3. Owen Young to M. H. Aylesworth, letter, November 16, 1926, ODY Papers, box 154, Advisory Council.

4. "Board Recommends First Code of Ethics," *NAB News*, February 27, 1928.

5. "NAB Code of Self Regulation, adopted July 11, 1939," *Broadcasting Yearbook, 1940*, Washington, DC: Broadcasting Publications, 1941.

6. *Red Lion Broadcasting Company v. FCC*, 395 U.S. 367.

7. FCC, *Memorandum Opinion and Order in Complaint of Syracuse Peace Council against Television Station WTVH*, 2 FCCRcd 5043, 5057–58.

8. See *Cruz v. Ferre*, 755 F.2d 1415 (11th Cir. 1985).

9. See *United States v. Playboy Entertainment Group*, 529 U.S. 803 (2000).

10. See *Reno v. American Civil Liberties Union*, 521 U.S. 844 (1997).

11. *Communications Act of 1934, as Amended*, 47 U.S.C.A. Section 315.

12. Benjamin, *Freedom of the Air*, 32–54 and 108–34.

13. *Farmers' Educational and Cooperative Union v. WDAY*, 360 U.S. 525 (1959).

14. Federal Election Campaign Act of 1971, Pub. L. No. 92–225, 86 Stat. 3 (1994), and *Communications Act of 1934, as Amended*, 47 U.S.C.A. Section 312(a)(7).

15. *CBS, Inc., v. FCC*, 453 U.S. 367 (1981).

16. Memorandum of minutes of the Advisory Council of the National Broadcasting Company, first meeting, February 1927, ODY Papers, box 154, Advisory Council.

Bibliography

Manuscript Collections

Archives of Industrial Society, University of Pittsburgh. Pittsburgh, Pennsylvania
    H. P. Davis Papers

AT&T Archives. Warren, New Jersey
    American Telephone and Telegraph Collection

Herbert Hoover Presidential Library. West Branch, Iowa
    Commerce Papers

Kansas State Libraries, Kansas State University. Manhattan, Kansas
    Francis D. Farrell Papers, Morse Department of Special Collections

Library of Congress. Washington, D.C.
    NBC Papers

National Archives. Washington, D.C.
    Federal Communications Commission Papers

Seely Mudd Library, Princeton University. Princeton, New Jersey
    ACLU Papers

St. Lawrence University Libraries. Canton, New York
    Owen D. Young Papers

Wisconsin State Historical Society Archives. Madison, Wisconsin
    Mass Communication Ephemera
    Martin Codel Collection
    National Broadcasting Company Papers

Library of American Broadcasting, University of Maryland. College Park, Maryland

Broadcast Pioneers Collection

National Association of Broadcasters Collection

Books and Articles

"Air Censorship on Birth Control Talks Assailed." New York *Herald Tribune*, January 17, 1930, n.p.

"Appeal by Air." Editorial. Washington *Post*, January 15, 1936.

Archer, Gleason. *History of Radio to 1926*. New York: American Historical Society, 1938.

Barfield, Ray. *Listening to Radio, 1920–1950*. Westport, CN: Praeger, 1996.

Barnouw, Erik. *A Tower in Babel: A History of Broadcasting in the United States to 1933*. New York: Oxford University Press, 1966.

Benjamin, Louise M. *Freedom of the Air and the Public Interest: First Amendment Rights in Broadcasting to 1935*. Carbondale: Southern Illinois University Press, 2001.

"Birth Control Group Criticizes Radio Ban." Buffalo *Evening News*, January 17, 1930, n.p.

"Board Recommends First Code of Ethics." *NAB News*, February 27, 1928.

Brinkley, Alan. *Voices of Dissent: Huey Long, Father Coughlin, and the Great Depression*. New York: Knopf, 1982.

"Broadcasters Plan Busy Days." New York *Times*, October 30, 1932, sec. 8, 6.

Brokenshire, Norman. *This Is Norman Brokenshire*. New York: McKay, 1954.

Butler, Jane. "The Case of Father Coughlin." Letter to the editor. *Christian Century*, March 23, 1932.

Butler, Paul, Jr. *Presidential Campaigns*. New York: Oxford University Press, 1985.

Cahalan, John, Jr. "The Hour of Power." *Commonweal*, January 28, 1931, 343–45.

"Campaign Expected to Aid Broadcasters." New York *Times*, March 11, 1928, sec. 9, 15.

"Campaign Wind-Up Upsets Radio Plans." New York *Times*, November 4, 1932, 11.

Case, Josephine, and Everett Case. *Owen D. Young and American Enterprise*. Boston: Godine, 1982.

Chapman, Richard A., ed. *The Role of Commissions in Policy-Making*. London: George Allen and Unwin, 1973.

Cochran, Leslie H., L. Allen Phelps, and Linda Letwin Cochran. *Advisory Committees in Action*. Boston: Allyn and Bacon, 1980.

Cole, Jacquelyn M., and Maurice F. Cole. *Advisory Councils: A Theoretical and Practical Guide for Program Planners*. Englewood Cliffs, NJ: Prentice-Hall, 1983.

Comora, Owen. "From McNamee to Huntley-Brinkley: 40 Years of Political Convention Broadcasting." *Electronic Age* 23, no. 3 (summer 1964).

"Coolidge Rebuff in Dill Radio Bill." New York *World*, May 7, 1926, n.p.

Communications Act of 1934, as Amended. 47 U.S.C.A. sections 312 (a)(7) and 315.

"Coughlin Condemns Our Policy in Mexico." New York *Times*, December 24, 1934, 9.

"Coughlin Puzzle, The." *Michigan Christian Advocate*, December 24, 1931, 5.

"Deplores 'Too Much Talk.'" New York *Times*, April 18, 1932, 17.

Douglas, George H. *The Early Days of Radio Broadcasting.* Jefferson, NC: McFarland, 1987.

"Dr. Parran Quits Council." New York *Times*, November 21, 1934, 20.

Dunlap, Orrin E., Jr. "Act II Begins." New York *Times*, January 17, 1937, 164.

———. "Elaborate Plans for Tuesday." New York *Times*, November 6, 1932, sec. 8, 6.

———. "Lessons of the Campaign." New York *Times*, November 13, 1932, sec. 8, 6.

———. "Two Hundred Broadcasters Join Convention Hook-Up," New York *Times*, June 12, 1932, sec. 9, 5.

———. "Voice of Victory, A." New York *Times*, November 8, 1936, X12.

Federal Communications Commission. *Mayflower Decision.* 8 FCC 333.

———. *Memorandum Opinion and Order in Complaint of Syracuse Peace Council against Television Station WTVH.* 2 FCCRcd 5043, 5057–58.

———. *Report on Chain Broadcasting.* Washington, DC: Government Printing Office, 1941.

"Final 'Words,' The." New York *Times*, October 25, 1936, X12.

Flinders, Matthew V., and Martin J. Smith, eds. *Quangos, Accountability, and Reform: The Politics of Quasi-Government.* New York: St. Martin's Press, 1999.

"G.O.P. Dramatizes What It Terms Dictatorship and Abuse of Relief." *Christian Science Monitor*, January 22, 1936, 8.

Gordon, L. *The Moral Property of Women: A History of Birth Control Politics in America.* 3d ed. Urbana: University of Illinois Press, 2002.

Hawley, Ellis. *The Great War and the Search for a Modern Order: A History of the American People and Their Institutions, 1917–1933.* New York: St. Martin's Press, 1979.

Head, Sydney. *Broadcasting in America: A Survey of Television and Radio.* Boston: Houghton Mifflin, 1956.

Hicks, John D. *The Republican Ascendency, 1921–1933.* New York: Harper and Row, 1960.

Hutchinson, Paul. "Is the Air Already Monopolized?" *Christian Century*, April 1, 1931, 441–44.

Jome, Hiram. *Economics of the Radio Industry.* Chicago: Shaw, 1925.

"Large Radio Chain in June for National Conclaves." New York *Times*, February 12, 1928, sec. 9, 14.

Lauter, Vita, and Joseph Friend. "Radio and the Censors." *Forum*, December 1931, 359–65.

"Leaders Point the Way to New Opportunities." New York *Times*, February 12, 1930, 12.

Leuchtenburg, William. *The Perils of Prosperity, 1914–32.* Chicago: University of Chicago Press, 1967.

Liberty at the Crossroads. January 8, 1936 (recording) RWC 6208, B2–3, NBC Collection, Library of Congress.

"Losers in Election Used Radio More." New York *Times*, December 10, 1936, 12.

"Mail Reveals American's Reaction to Politics on the Air." New York *Times*, July 17, 1932, sec. 8, 5.

McCann, C. R. *Birth Control Politics in the United States, 1916–1945.* Ithaca, NY: Cornell University Press, 1994.

McCoy, Donald. *Coming of Age.* Middlesex, UK: Penguin, 1973.

McNamee, Graham. "The Elephant and the Donkey Take the Air." *American Magazine*, November 1928, 15.

Mueller, Robert K. *The Director's and Officer's Guide to Advisory Boards.* New York: Quorum, 1990.

"NAB Code of Self Regulation, Adopted July 11, 1939." *Broadcasting Yearbook, 1940*, Washington, DC: Broadcasting Publications, 1941.

Nash, Gerald. *The Great Transition.* Boston: Allyn and Bacon, 1971.

"New Deal Assailed." Washington *Post*, February 5, 1936, 7.

"$1,000,000 on Air for G.O.P." New York *Times*, January 13, 1936, 2.

"Party Head Reveals Ban." New York *Times*, January 14, 1936, 17.

"Personal Touch Survives." New York *Times*, October 29, 1932, 14.

"Politics Irks Broadcasters." New York *Times*, October 23, 1932, sec. 8, 6.

"Politics on Air Ousts Regular Programs." New York *Times*, November 2, 1934, 16.

"Preparing for the Crusade." New York *Times*, September 4, 1932.

"President Employs Air, Press to Educate Nation." *Literary Digest*, January 27, 1934, 9.

"Priest Defends His Radio Talks." New York *Times*, May 10, 1932, 23.

"Protests Radio Chain Ban." New York *Times*, November 26, 1929, n.p.

"Radio and the New Oratory." Editorial. *Christian Century*, November 30, 1932, 146.

"Radio 'Debunking' the Campaigns." *Literary Digest*, December 1, 1928.

"Radio Prepares for Barrage on Political Oratory." New York *Times*, June 5, 1932, sec. 10, 8.

"Radio to Elect Next President." *Christian Science Monitor*, February 26, 1936.

"Roosevelt and Cabinet." New York *Times*, December 24, 1934, 9.

"Roosevelt Bars Radio in Talk to Bankers; To Keep Broadcasts for 'Fireside Chats.'" New York *Times*, October 9, 1934, 2.

Rorty, J. "The Impending Radio War." *Harper's Monthly Magazine* 163 (November 1931), 725.

Rosen, Philip. *The Modern Stentors*. Westport, CN: Greenwood Press, 1980.

Ryan, Quin. "Quin Ryan Recalls Early Conventions." Chicago *Tribune*, July 12, 1964, radio sec., 10.

Sarnoff, David. "Principles and Practices of Network Radio Broadcasting." Hearings before the Federal Communications Commission, November 14, 1938.

Shepard, William G. "Blotting Out the Blah." *Collier's*, August 23, 1924.

Skelcher, Chris. *The Appointed State: Quasi-governmental Organizations and Democracy*. Buckingham, UK: Open University Press, 1998.

Smith, Stephanie. *Federal Advisory Committees: A Primer*. New York: Novinka, 2002.

Sterling, Christopher, and John Michael Kittross. *Stay Tuned: A History of American Broadcasting*. 3rd ed. Mahwah, NJ: Erlbaum, 2002.

Summers, Harrison B., and Worth McDougald. *Programming on Radio and Television*. 2nd ed. Athens, GA: University of Georgia, 1959.

"Today's Town Crier." Editorial. New York *Times*, November 6, 1930, 24.

U.S. Census, Bureau of Economic Analysis. Table 657. Selected Per Capita Income and Product Items in Current and Real (2000) Dollars: 1929 to 2006.

U.S. Congress, House of Representatives. "To Regulate Radio Communication and for Other Purposes." Hearings before the Committee on the Merchant Marine and Fisheries on H.R. 7357. 68th Congress, first session.

"World Will Hear Inaugural Events." New York *Times*, January 20, 1937, 9.

Legal Cases

CBS, Inc., v. FCC. 453 U.S. 367 (1981).

Cruz v. Ferre. 755 F2d 1415 (11th Cir. 1985).

Duncan v. U.S. 48 F2d 128 (1931).

Farmers' Educational and Cooperative Union v. WDAY. 360 U.S. 525 (1959).

FCC v. Pacifica Foundation. 438 U.S. 726, 727–28 (1978).

Federal Election Campaign Act of 1971. Pub. L. No. 92–225, 86 Stat. 3 (1994).

KFKB Broadcasting Assn., Inc., v. FRC. 47 F2d 670 (1931).

Red Lion Broadcasting Company v. FCC, 395 U.S. 367 (1969).

Reno v. American Civil Liberties Union, 521 U.S. 844 (1997).

Trinity Methodist Church, South, v. FRC, 62 F2d 850 (1932).

United States v. Playboy Entertainment Group, 529 U.S. 803 (2000).

Index

ABCL. *See* American Birth Control League (ABCL)

ABC network, 111–12

adult education, trends in, 47

advertisers and radio, 9, 24–25, 32

advisory councils, 11, 14–15. *See also* NBC Advisory Council

affiliate stations: and agricultural programs, 31; average broadcast day at, 86; and controversial issues of public importance, 101; in late 1920s and early 1930s, 43, 79, 82; and sustaining programs, 85

AFL (American Federation of Labor), 20–21

Agricultural Adjustment Administration (AAA), 37, 86

agricultural press, 34

agricultural programs: affiliate stations for, 31; *Farm Forum*, 36; government agencies and, 33; *NBC Farm Forum*, 34–35, 37; *Western Farm and Home Hour*, 36–37. See also *Farm and Home Hour*; *National Farm and Home Hour*

agriculture committee, 24, 28

airtime: charges for, 77, 80, 84; for commercial vs. sustaining programs, 32

Alderman, Edwin, 19, 22, 24, 43–44, 105–6

American Agriculture Mobilizes (radio program), 40

American Birth Control League (ABCL), 31, 53, 67–68, 73–74

American broadcasting, characteristics of, 87

American Civil Liberties Union (ACLU), 55–56, 69, 77–78

American Federation of Labor (AFL), 20–21

American Library Association, 44

American Red Cross, 42

American Socialist Party, 74, 76–77, 84, 97

American society, tensions over changing lifestyles and customs in, 48–49

Amos 'n' Andy (radio program), 7, 88

Angell, James, 40, 59, 63, 103, 105–6

anti-Semitism by Father Coughlin, 58

Arlin, Harold W., 1

ASCAP-BMI controversy, 110

AT&T, 4–6

audiences: of *Farm and Home Hour*, 35; general, 7–8; of *Golden Hour of the Little Flower*, 54; live, compared with radio, 62; of *Music Appreciation Hour*, 42; rural, 27–29, 36

Aylesworth, Merlin: and Advisory Council formation and composition, 14–15; on airtime for commercial vs. sustaining programs, 32; as ex-officio member of NBC Advisory Council, 87; and *Farm and Home Hour*, 29; on FDR's use of radio, 86; on NBC's attempts at evenhandedness, 87–88; on NBC's election coverage, 78–81, 85; on NBC's public service, 30; on NBC's rejection of birth control program, 72; and opera broadcasts, 46; on political education programs, 78; and prize for jazz compositions, 43; on religious programming, 50; and Rutherford's protest, 51–52

Democratic Party, 84, 97
Division of Talks, 106
documentary dramatizations, 89–90, 93–94
dramatic programs, 7–8, 25
dramatic sketches in *National Farm and Home Hour*, 34
dramatization of political issues, 89–90, 93–94

Edgar Bergen and Charlie McCarthy Show, 103
educational programming, 43, 46, 50, 78, 99, 105–6
education committee, 24, 28, 44
equal opportunities doctrine, 77–79, 96
equitable coverage issue, 86, 106
"Essay on the Principle of Population, An" (Peck), 68
eugenics, 66–67
European broadcasting, characteristics of, 87
evening programming, 7, 38, 113
evolution, 67

Fairness Doctrine, 107, 117
Farley, James, 94–95
Farm and Home Hour: on Blue Network, 38; coast-to-coast network airing of, 31; daily weather forecast, 33–34; nonagricultural organizations and, 35; programming in 1933, 37–38; publicity for *Music Appreciation Hour* on, 34; reaching rural audiences through, 36; as sustaining program, 114–15; World War II and, 40–41. See also *National Farm and Home Hour*
farm economic crisis, 26
farmers, and program evolution, 7
Farm Forum, 36. See also *NBC Farm Forum*
farm relief, 26–27
Farrell, Francis D.: on agricultural programming, 33–34, 47; and agriculture committee, 24, 28; in debate over public demand in broadcast decisions, 73; and *Farm and Home Hour*, 29, 31, 36–38; on *Farm Forum*, 37; on free speech, 62; and *National Farm and Home Hour*, 30–31, 38–39; on policies regarding religious programs, 63; selection of, for NBC Advisory Council, 19; on sponsored programs with news commentators, 101; and sponsorship controversy, 40; on Starch Reports, 30
FCC. See Federal Communications Commission (FCC)
feature programs, 28
Federal Communications Commission (FCC): complaint to, by Carter-Mondale commit-

tee, 119; and Fairness Doctrine, 117; and FRC program policies, 88; letter campaign on behalf of Father Coughlin, 57; and *Mayflower* decision, 106–7; network monopoly investigation, 110; and political coverage, 118; and shortwave broadcasting, 102
Federal Election Campaign Act (1971), 118
Federal Radio Commission (FRC): and acceptable program practices, 115; early work of, 9; and Father Coughlin, 54, 56; inquiry into commercialism and education in radio, 44; on program censorship, 69–70; Radio Act of 1927 and, 69; survey of radio programming, 49
Federal Trade Commission (FTC), 4–5
feminists, 66–67, 75
fireside chats, 86
"Food for Freedom" campaign, 40
foreign events, radio reporting of, 108
foreign immigration, and perceived social decline, 65
FRC. See Federal Radio Commission (FRC)
free speech on radio, 60–62, 68–69, 100, 103–4
FTC (Federal Trade Commission), 4–5

General Electric (GE), 3–5
Golden Hour of the Little Flower (radio program), 54
Goodyear Tire and Rubber Company, 39
government agencies, and agricultural broadcasting, 33
great books program, 45
Great Depression, 27, 34–36, 81–82, 86
"Great Messages of Religion," 50
Green, William: and committee to select liberal individual, 32; on complaint by Watch Tower Society, 53; on coverage of labor issues, 86; in debate over public demand in broadcast decisions, 73; on educational programming, 106; and labor committee, 24; on NBC programming, 28–29; and policies on religious broadcasting, 63; on Rutherford and People's Pulpit Association, 52; selection of, for NBC Advisory Council, 20–21

Harbord, J. G., 12, 112
Hard, William, 83–84
Harding, Warren, 26–27
homemakers, in program evolution, 7
honoraria for NBC Advisory Council members, 24, 111, 114
Hoover, Herbert, 77, 80, 82–84

Hughes, Charles Evans, 15–17, 31, 52, 72–74, 115
human interest programs, 8
Hutchins, Robert Maynard, 44–47, 87–88

Ickes, Harold, 102
instructor's manuals, 42–44
international agricultural events, 33
Internet content, control of, 118
interviews in broadcasting, 35

Jazz Age, 49
Jewish organizations and religious program-
    ming, 54
Jews, and WASP superiority, 49
Johnson, Hugh S., 63, 101
Johnson, Tom Loftin, 31–32
Johnson-Long-Coughlin controversy, 88
Julius Rosenwald Fund, 18

Kaltenborn, H. V., 83
KDKA radio, 1
KVEP radio, Portland, Oregon, 82

Labor and Democracy (Green), 21
labor committee, 24
League of Nations, 17
League of Women Voters, 78
lecture programs, 28. See also speeches
letters from listeners, 35–36, 41–42, 54, 83
libel laws, 62, 82
Liberty at the Crossroads (RNC): broadcast of,
    by WGN in Chicago, 96–98; NBC Advisory
    Council consideration of, 95–96; NBC's and
    CBS's reaction to, 93–95; as negative pro-
    gram-length commercials, 89–90; skits in,
    90–92, 96–97
license revocations, 82, 118
license term, 103
Literary Digest, 15
Lohr, Lenox: on allotting time for opposing
    views, 63; on controversial issues of public
    importance, 100–101; on FCC oversight,
    62; on freedom of the air, 103–4; on Liberty
    at the Crossroads, 93; and NBC Advisory
    Council, 59; on NBC policies on political
    programming, 95; and NBC policies on
    religious programs, 103; and NBC's policies
    on political programming, 89; as speaker
    on National Farm and Home Hour, 39; and
    sponsorship controversy, 40
Long, Huey, 63, 88
Lundborg, F. L., 63, 101

MacFarland, Charles F.: and church activities
    committee, 24; and Committee on Religious
    Activities, 48; in debate over public demand
    in broadcast decisions, 73; guidelines for re-
    ligious programs, 63; resignation of, 31; selec-
    tion of, for NBC Advisory Council, 17–18
Major Barbara (Shaw), 89
man-on-the-street programs, 9
Marconi Company, 3
Mayflower decision, 106
McNamee, Graham, 79–80
Message of Israel (radio program), 57
Metropolitan Opera, 89
military crisis, potential role of radio in, 108–9
Miller, Neville, 60–61
monopolistic practices, allegations of, 4–7
Montgomery Ward, 29
moral relativism, 48–49
Morrow, Dwight W., 20–21, 44
Mullen, Frank, 29–31, 34–37
music and culture committee, 24
Music Appreciation Hour: basis for, 29; Dam-
    rosch and, 20; farm economic crisis and, 26;
    in-classroom use, 41–42; as model for edu-
    cational programming, 46; NBC Advisory
    Council and, 10; origins of, 25; publicity for,
    on Farm and Home Hour, 34; as sustaining
    program, 114–15
music programming, 25, 33, 46–47, 99, 109–10

National Advisory Council on Radio in Educa-
    tion (NACRE), 43–44
National Association of Broadcasters (NAB),
    60–61, 76, 110, 115
National Broadcasting Company. See NBC (Na-
    tional Broadcasting Company)
National Democratic Committee, 84
National Farm and Home Hour: in 1930, 33–34;
    farm economic crisis and, 26; first broadcast
    of, 30–31; increased use of, to reach rural au-
    diences, 36; NBC Advisory Council and, 10;
    origins of, 25; sponsorship controversy, 39–
    40; three-thousandth program of, 38–39
National Federation of Music Clubs, 42
national radio network: in 1930, 32; concerns
    over, and creation of Advisory Council,
    11–14; expansion of, in Midwest and West,
    27–28; program evolution through 1945, 8–9;
    temporary coast-to-coast system, 5–6
National Recovery Administration (NRA)
    codes, 86
Navy, U.S., 3–4

public demand in broadcast decisions, 73; and political education programs, 78; on scheduling of women's programs, 105; selection of, for NBC Advisory Council, 20–22; as welfare feminist, 75; and women's activities committee, 24

shortwave radio, 83, 102, 104

Sixty Families, The (Lundborg), 101

skits, in *Liberty at the Crossroads*, 90–92, 96–97

Smith, Al, 58–59, 80, 97, 103, 110

soap operas, 8, 113

Socialist Party, 74, 76–77, 84, 97

social mores in 1920s, 48–49

song-and-patter teams, 7

speeches: in 1932 programming, 35; political, 77–78, 83–84, 97; presidential, 93–95

sponsored programs, 9, 39–40, 101, 103, 114

sponsors, and controversial issues of public importance, 101

Spoul, C. A., 109

Starch Reports, 30

station announcements, 9

stock market crash, 27

strip programming, 8, 113

Studebaker, John W., 102

Summerall, Charles, 22

superpower stations in network structure, 12

sustaining programs, 9, 32, 85, 100–101, 103–4

syphilis control, censorship of references to, 67

taboo subjects, 65

talk radio, 25, 117

taxes on corporate profits, 10

teachers' manuals for *Music Appreciation Hour*, 41–44

telephone giveaway programs, 9

Telephone Group, 5–6

television demonstration, 110

third parties, 78–79

Thomas, Norman, 55, 80–81, 84; 61–62

thriller dramas, 9

Town Hall Meeting of the Air, 62

Trammell, Niles, 110–12

Tripp, Guy, 20–21, 27

Truth or Consequences (radio program), 8

Tweed, William "Boss," 17

Tyson, Levering, 43–44

"Uncle Sam's Forest Rangers" (radio program), 34

United Fruit Company, 4–5

United Mine Workers of America, 20–21

University of Chicago Press, 44

University of Minnesota, 74

University of the Air, 50

U.S. Department of Agriculture (USDA), 29–30, 34, 37, 39–40

U.S. Department of Interior, 35

U.S. Postal Service, 35

variety programs, 8, 25

Victorian era, 74

vignettes, in *Liberty at the Crossroads*, 90–92, 96–97

WABC radio, 84

Wallace, Henry, 39

Warburg, Felix, 44–45, 100

Warburg, Frieda (Schiff), 45

Warburg, Paul, 45

Ward, Harry, 69, 71, 73–74

Washington *Post*, 94

WASP (white Anglo-Saxon Protestant) superiority, 49

Watch Tower Bible and Tract Society (People's Pulpit Association), 51–54

Watson, James, 77–78

WDAY case, 118

welfare feminists, 66–67, 75

West, Mae, 103

Western Farm and Home Hour, 33, 36–37

Westinghouse, and patent pooling, 4–5

WEVD radio, 74

WGN radio, Chicago, 96

WGY radio, Schenectady, 52

What's on the Air (digest of radio programs), 41

Wheeler, Burton, 61, 77–78

Wile, F. W., 83–84

Williams, Lynn A., 45

Willis, Frank, 79

Wilson, Woodrow, 32, 97

wired miles, 43

WJR radio, Detroit, 55–56

WJZ radio, 1

WLS radio, 31

WLW radio, Cincinnati, 77–78

WMAQ radio, 29

women's activities committee, 24

women's club mentality, 75

women's daytime serial dramas (soap operas), 8, 113

World Court (Permanent Court of International Justice), 17